John Charles Carrick

The story of the burning bush

A simple narrative of the Church of Scotland

John Charles Carrick

The story of the burning bush
A simple narrative of the Church of Scotland

ISBN/EAN: 9783743342040

Manufactured in Europe, USA, Canada, Australia, Japa

Cover: Foto ©Lupo / pixelio.de

Manufactured and distributed by brebook publishing software (www.brebook.com)

John Charles Carrick

The story of the burning bush

STORY OF THE BURNING BUSH.

THE STORY

OF

THE BURNING BUSH.

A SIMPLE NARRATIVE OF THE CHURCH
OF SCOTLAND.

BY

THE REV. J. C. CARRICK, B.D., F.S.A. SCOT.
MINISTER OF NEWBATTLE.

EDINBURGH:
JAMES G. HITT, 37 GEORGE STREET.
1890.

PREFATORY NOTE.

THE following sketches were prepared with a strictly practical end in view, and make no claim to literary finish or artistic grace. The writer's single wish and aim has been to increase the devotion of the people towards the Ancient Church of the Country, whose expressive crest and symbol the Burning Bush has been for at least two centuries.

CONTENTS.

CHAPTER I.
	PAGE
HOW SCOTLAND WAS BROUGHT TO THE FOOT OF THE CROSS	9

CHAPTER II.
SCOTLAND ENROLLED AS A PROVINCE OF CHRIST'S EMPIRE	19

CHAPTER III.
UNDER THE SHADOW OF ST PETER'S	27

CHAPTER IV.
THE DECLINE AND FALL OF ROME	39

CHAPTER V.
A NEW PHŒNIX ARISES OUT OF THE ASHES OF THE OLD	48

CHAPTER VI.
A SCOTTISH HILDEBRAND	57

CHAPTER VII.
DARK DAYS	65

CONTENTS.

CHAPTER VIII.

	PAGE
"Nec Tamen Consumebatur".	74

CHAPTER IX.

Peace with Honour	84

CHAPTER X.

"And the Land had Rest"	93

CHAPTER XI.

"That They all may be One"	103

CHAPTER XII.

"Forward in the Name of God"	111

THE STORY OF THE BURNING BUSH.

CHAPTER I.

HOW SCOTLAND WAS BROUGHT TO THE FOOT OF THE CROSS.

"WHEN your children shall ask their fathers in time to come, saying, What mean ye by these stones? then ye shall let the children of Israel *know.*" So spake Joshua to the Hebrew children at Jordan. No matter how brilliant the event, or deed, or personage, the lapse of time will wear the remembrance out, as the rain wears the lettering off a tombstone. A generation will arise that knew not Joseph, and if the memory of Joseph is to be preserved, the facts of Joseph's character and life must be repeated and lived over again.

Every few miles in Scotland you come to a little pile of gray, old, weather-beaten, rain-worn stones, from which springs a stone finger pointing heavenwards. It is the "God's-Place" (the fine old Scottish word for a church) of the parish, and the green God's-Acre spreads around it. It is the spiritual hearth-stone, where the earthly children meet the Great All-Father; it is there that you see the marks of where the heavenly ladder rests, by which man's stumbling soul can rise up on steeps of light to the Infinite.

Some of these stones are older,—some newer; in some cases, the *stone pillow,* on which, Jacob-like, the wearied spirit lays down its head to rest, and where, thank God, it has so often found it; in some cases the pillow is sorely worn; in a few cases, as at Iona and Melrose, altogether worn out; in other cases, it is fresh and new, with little history behind it. But the great mass of our Scottish churches and cathedrals are the children of long ago. The spiritual hearth-stone in each parish has been lying there, as a rule, for many long centuries, and has warmed countless generations; it has lain, like the philosopher's stone of old, transforming dust and ashes into golden lives, changing men, Galatea-like, from dead cold mortal clay, into heavenly beauty and spiritual perfection!

It is a little sad to think, that while the power is happily denied them, the wish is very present in the hearts of some, who have been reared and nourished in these mother-churches, to put their Mother to death, to quench these spiritual hearths where they themselves were warmed into being, to raze the stones which the fathers of old laid, in remembrance of God's goodness, and to cover his spiritual family for ages to come with the shelter of a true and pure religion. To them the stone in which good men for ages in Scotland have taken pleasure, is, not a *load-stone* to attract, but a *stumbling-stone* and a rock of offence.

They point to younger and, as they aver, more vigorous churches. They point to the *growths* of ages which have accumulated over the stones of our National Zion, forgetting that there are some worse growths than the lichen-growths of age, namely the fungus, mushroom growths of fell disease. They have even the bad taste to draw attention to the irregular hewing and eccentricities of some of the stones, squared and laid by far better hands than either theirs or ours, cemented, too, to a great extent with blood,—a moral error as grievous and offensive as that of the son who treats his mother lightly because she has wrinkles and white hair, and because, having now his young blue puppy-eyes opened to know good and evil, he imagines that even when younger (before he was born), she might have been better looking, and marvels at his father's choice of so plain a bride!

"When your chimney has smoked as long as ours, it will perhaps need sweeping too," is the right and the famous reply. There is only *one kind of sweeping* which we do not wish—*sweeping away!* There is no true Scottish Churchman to-day, who is not ready and most anxious to see the many abuses in the Church remedied, and additional attractions and beauties added to the *Old House!* "Her saints take pleasure in her stones: her very dust to them is dear;" yes, but we want the stones of stumbling taken away, and the dust of decay and carelessness and death swept out. But, before you cry with the heathen of old, "Raze it, raze it," sit down and think! Destruction is easy; construction is difficult. Dog Diamond can undo in a moment what Philosopher Newton took a lifetime to effect. Ask what it is that you are invited to drop like Cleopatra's pearl, worth a kingdom, into the bitter acid wine-cup of ecclesiastical controversy, to be melted and lost for ever! Take a good practical look at the pearl before you part with it, lest when you have taken it out of your bosom, and parted with it, you find that you have reversed the conduct of the merchantman of Scripture, and *lost the pearl of great price*, to find yourself landed with a multitudinous *handful of dim and inferior gems.*

The object of my short, plain, and unpretending "Story of the Burning Bush," is to answer the query with which I began, and to give a reply to the general question which is being asked on every side in the Northern Kingdom— "What mean ye by these stones?" also to show how well worthy the Church of Scotland is of preservation, and of that great tide of success which has, during the last few years, turned upon her,—by climbing the Hill of History, and looking back on all the way by which Almighty God has led her, from her cradle in sea-washed, storm-swept Iona, to the present hour, blessed as she is with more than half a million sworn and staunch members, and, with the exception of a handful of noisy malcontents, the good wishes and benison of the entire Scottish people.

The story is a long one, for the Church of Scotland is more than one thousand three hundred years old; and it is a peculiar and difficult one to tell, for there have been many ups and downs, and controversies and divisions: as the old chronicler Wyntoun puts it—"The Church of Scotland always *loved a way of its own.*" From first to last, the Scottish *character* has been amply illustrated in the history of the Scottish Kirk—independent, determined, fearless, a little self-willed, straight. But, with all these phases, the Church never suffered eclipse. There is a distinct organic unity all through: the Church of Scotland to-day is simply the Church of the early Christian centuries, grown up and developed.

How was Scotland brought to the foot of the Cross? How was the lamp of Christ's Church lit in this land of gross darkness, contemptuously called by some Southerners, "The knuckle-end of England"? It may be the knuckle-end, but it is a knuckle which the wide world regards with deep respect, and of which the enemy, material or spiritual, has a very wholesome dread. Beware of the knuckle!

For long after the Romans had conquered Britain, the Caledonians of the North remained independent and unvanquished. The Roman soldiers seemed to have formed a terrible estimate of the courage and fierceness of our ancient forefathers. Across Northumberland they built the Hadrian Wall, to preserve the South from the Caledonian inroads; and further up, joining the Firths of Forth and Clyde, the Antonine Wall or "Graham's Dyke," to act as a second barrier. And these two huge stone masses, the fragments of which still survive, were intended as a pair of gigantic handcuffs to hold down the fierce prisoner. Up till the end of the fourth century, while Roman camps, and forts, and roads were to be found north of this upper check, the people still remained free and unsubdued, till Rome had at last to give up the task in despair. About the beginning of the fifth century all the troops were withdrawn from these parts, to defend the heart of the Empire, Eternal Rome, against the invading Goths, who were then thundering at her gates.

HOW SCOTLAND WAS BROUGHT TO THE FOOT OF THE CROSS. 13

Long after the Roman legions had carried their eagles away, and had sailed off in their galleys and settled down again in sunny Italy—when listening on the cold winter nights to the long howling of the wolves outside, and the shriek of the Apennine tempest, and the merry crackling of the red logs on the hearth, strange weird memories came back to these old soldiers, as they recalled the fearful fights they had waged long ago at the Scottish walls, away up in " Ultima Thule," and with a shiver they conjured up the gloom and darkness and mist that rolled away into nothingness, and got mingled with the massy granite mountains looming solemnly beyond the great stone barrier. And the old sentry lived over again the days, when on the summit of one of the Wall-Forts, shading his eyes with his hand, he peered out from under his helmet into the unknown lands beyond.

Here is a description of Caledonia by a Greek writer of the sixth century, whose information evidently came from the reports of Cæsar's returned legions. "On the North side of the Wall of Hadrian, all is different, insomuch that it would be impossible for a man to live there, even for half an hour. Vipers and serpents innumerable, with all other kinds of wild beasts, infest that place. And, what is most strange, the natives affirm that if any one passing that Wall should proceed to the other side, he would die immediately—unable to endure the unwholesomeness of the atmosphere; death also attacking such beasts as go thither, destroys them. They say that the souls of men departed are always conducted to this place, but in what manner I will explain immediately, having frequently heard it from men of that region, relating it most seriously."

Is it not rather strange to read these words of the Byzantine historian, Procopius, reproducing the awe-struck sentiments of the Roman sentry on the Scottish Wall, as he peered out into the dim unknown land? A land to-day possessed of two great cities, one of which rivals Rome in population, and the other, Athens in culture. But such were their views of poor Scotland; and so, wearied of the constant feud with the indomitable Picts, the Roman eagles went south and made way for the standard of the Cross—and the soldiers of Cæsar were supplanted by the soldiers of Christ.

No sooner did the legions leave than the missioners of Jesus arrived: and what Rome with all its power could not effect, the peaceful faith of Christ accomplished, and savage Scotland which had set its teeth against Cæsar's spearmen and archers, threw its soul at the feet of Emmanuel. "Nazarene," as the Emperor Julian said on dying, feeling himself powerless against the calm power of the religion of peace and goodwill, and unable to do what it could do— "Thou hast conquered!" "'Εν τουτῳ νικα," to echo the other church legend—" in this (the Cross of Christ), thou shalt be victorious!"

The earliest spark of Christianity in Scotland was kindled at its extreme south point, at Whithorn in Wigtonshire, or, as the old name was, Whitherne in Galloway. The Roman legions gone, the Picts again pressed on the South, and were over-riding all the North of England. In 420 A.D., a monk, St Ninian, or St Ninias, a native of North Wales, where the British Church was flourishing vigorously, penetrated up into the country of the Southern Picts, Yorkshire, and the Northern counties, and finally, cross in hand, and heart on fire with love to God and man, crossed the Solway, and landed at Whitherne, where, after a time, he built the first Christian Church in Scotland, made of polished freestone; and, therefore, this small cathedral, the ecclesiastical centre of North England, and as yet, of the whole of Scotland, was called "Candida Casa," or "White House," hence *Whitherne*, because of the bright polish of its stones. St Ninian had it raised into an Episcopal See, and soon it was a great centre of Christian activity amongst the Southern Picts. This early Pictish Cathedral seems to have been of remarkable beauty and striking stateliness, judging from the fame of it which history has brought down.

It was therefore on the stormy Solway coast that Christ's

lamp was first lit in Scotland; and in course of time it cast the gospel radiance over a wide tract of country on both sides of the firth.

A hundred years passed away, and Jesus was again seen walking amid the candlesticks, and lighting the second lamp in this land. It was in Clydesdale at Glasgow; and the human agent was St Kentigern, or as he is generally called, St Mungo (the Beloved Disciple), a name given him by his master.

He was a Pict, and therefore well fitted to move his own countrymen. He was a pupil of St Serf, and at the beginning of the sixth century he pressed up, carrying the gospel torch in his hand, into the dark heathen region of the West of Scotland, where, by his zeal and holiness, he won the race over to Christ's faith, and the heathen wilderness was gradually transformed into the garden of the Lord. But in 543 A.D. a usurper came to the throne of North Britain and expelled the saint, so that he fled to Wales, and there lived for a few years with St David and St Asaph. After all danger was past, he, with a little band of missionaries, journeyed back again to Scotland, and settled down at Glasgow, building a wooden church on the banks of the Clyde, the site of which has for ages been covered by that "sermon in stone," and petrified anthem, the glorious minster of St Mungo, built by the offerings of universal christendom; and whose crypt, with its dim pillared calm, Prince Albert declared to be the finest thing of the kind in the world. The whole district which the vast city of Glasgow now covers was once clothed with a primeval forest, in which Druidical rites were celebrated. Some Druidical relics have been from time to time discovered within the cathedral precincts. The name "Glasgow" means "the dark forest." St Kentigern cut down a great part of these woods, and taught the people agriculture, and supplanted the gross rites of the Druids with the worship of the Cross.

From this centre missionaries were sent forth to the

extreme north of Scotland, to the Orkneys, to Norway, and even to Iceland. St Mungo's monument still exists in Glasgow Cathedral, and it was at this shrine that Edward I. made offerings, and that Robert Bruce did penance after the murder of the Red Comyn. St Mungo's well is still springing in the crypt of the magnificent minster of the west. The city arms of Glasgow preserve the tradition of what is reported as his great miracle, which concerned one of the early Scottish Queens, who gave her signet-ring to a favourite knight. The king saw this knight asleep one day with the ring on his finger, and slipped it off the unconscious hand, and threw it into the river. He then charged the queen with not having the ring. In her despair she implored St Mungo to recover it; and at his bidding a salmon brought it up from the bed of the Clyde. Hence "the salmon with the ring in its mouth." The *tree* is a reminiscence of the great Glasgow forest, of which the Clydesdale orchards are but a puny remnant; and the *bell* refers to the famous Great Tom of Glasgow Cathedral, which had no small renown. "Glasgow for bells," was the old proverb!

The third lamp of Christianity, and by far the brightest and clearest of them all—so much so, that it can almost be said that, until then, the "Light of the World" hardly shone at all across Scotland, was kindled in Iona island by St Columba about the year 563 A.D. Columba was an Irishman, and born at Gartan, in Donegal, in 521. He was a scion of an ancient Irish royal house, and in early youth entered the monastery of Clonard in Meath, under St Patrick's guidance. Having offended an Irish king, he sailed across the channel with a band of missionary monks, in small wicker boats called coracles, and after a stormy voyage, arrived at the little isle of Hy or Iona, away out in the bleak Atlantic, off the coast of Mull.

When he arrived, only the southern parts of Scotland were Christian, the great mass of the country being still sunk in heathenism. When he died in 597, Scotland was lying at the foot of the Cross, and a hundred religious houses, besides several hundred churches, were dotted all over the West and North, the names and sites of many of which still survive in tradition, as monuments of his stupendous labours.

Dr Johnson in a famous sentence declares that he does not envy the man whose patriotism is not quickened at Marathon, and whose devotion is not stimulated at Iona. Wonderful is it to think of so bright a light having shone out to all Scotland, and even to the whole of Europe, from that bleak, inhospitable bit of rocky island,—the child of Old Ocean, the breakwater of the Atlantic waves.

"Small and mean though this island is," said St Columba on dying, "it shall be held in great and unusual honour, not only by Scottish kings and people, but also by the rulers of foreign and barbarous nations and by their subjects; the saints also, even of other churches, shall regard it with no common reverence." It was St Columba who led Scotland by the hand, like a little child, to Jesus; and he well deserves the name of "The Apostle of Scotland." To him we owe it that to-day, in every few miles of country, you find the little pile of sacred stones I spoke of at the beginning, with the heaven-directed finger, holding up a gilded cross to a world's admiration. His hand struck the match on the cold altar-stone of Iona Cathedral, from which the whole great candlestick of Scottish Christianity has been lighted.

It is touching to visit Iona, and to see how the simple people even yet venerate his memory, now more than 1300 years' old. On certain nights of the year, they declare his shadowy form is to be seen standing on the top of the ruined little cathedral of the Isles, counting the surrounding islands which he brought to Christ, to see that none have been carried away by the evil power. And there is a strong conviction in the minds of many in the Highlands, that Iona will yet again be, as it was in the days of old, the centre of Christianity for Scotland and Western Europe, and that its captivity will yet be turned. There is a prophecy to this effect in an ancient Latin hymn, by St Columba, called the "Altus," still extant, and lately translated by the Marquis of Bute. So holy was the ground considered, that all the early Scottish kings were buried in I-colm-kill, "St Columb's isle." In the burial ground no less than fifty-five kings lie sleeping, forty-two of Scotland, four of Ireland, eight of Norway, and one of France. Learned men and saints from all parts of the world visited this Holy Isle, from which was sent forth "the light to lighten the Gentiles." "Surely the isles have waited for Him."

Here is the translation of an ancient Gaelic prophecy of the future glory of Iona :—

> "Seven years before that awful day
> When time shall be no more,
> A watery deluge will o'er-sweep
> Hibernia's mossy shore.
>
> The green-clad Isla, too, shall sink
> When with the great and good,
> Columba's happy isle will rear
> Her towers above the flood!"

And thus Scotland was brought to the foot of the Cross; and thus St Columba proved to Scotland the spiritual "Dove" (as his name implies) coming over the wild waters, carrying the Olive branch of Christ's Peace and God's salvation to those who sat in darkness, and beckoning on others to follow him into the ark of the Church. Thus the Burning Bush was kindled in the land of the Thistle, and thus the ancient church of Scotland "was founded" literally "upon the floods."

CHAPTER II.

SCOTLAND ENROLLED AS A PROVINCE OF CHRIST'S EMPIRE.

Culdee Period: 600—1100 A.D.

ON Easter Eve, a very impressive ceremony takes place in the Greek Church, which regards the commemoration of Christ's Resurrection as the greatest and most solemn event of the Christian year. Throughout Russia, Greece, and the East generally, the churches and cathedrals begin to get thronged about ten o'clock on the Saturday night, and each worshipper brings with him a single candle or taper, and goes in and kneels down to pray. The whole church is in darkness, save for one small light which flickers mysteriously in the sanctuary, above the altar, casting long black shadows all over the sombre church and prostrate congregation. The vast throng is waiting in anxious expectancy for the resurrection morn. There is not a light, not a sound (as an eye-witness of the scene in the cathedral at Athens describes it), and each individual of the crowd remains motionless: a feeling of gloom and despair broods over every heart. As midnight approaches, the Archbishop and his attendants, with the King and Queen of Greece, go up and stand near the darkened altar, at which one of the priests murmurs a melancholy chant in low whispers. Suddenly as the hour of midnight is boomed out from the cathedral belfry into the still night air, a sharp report of a cannon bursts over the city, and the old archbishop lifting up his hands cries aloud to the congregation—"Christ is risen!" At the same moment he lights his taper at the crimson altar-lamp, and from his candle the priests light their tapers, and hand on the flame to the people; and so from hand to hand the fire spreads until every worshipper is marked out with a spark, and the whole cathedral is illuminated with a perfect blaze of lights. And so amid thousands of gleaming tapers and strains of the most enchanting music, the Easter cry of Alleluia is raised, and the sorrow and darkness are turned into joy and light, for "the Lord is risen indeed!"

Behind this ancient ritual there lurks a beautiful figure of the spread of Christianity throughout the world. From Christ's rocky tomb, the first light was struck: from it, the countless lamps of Christendom have been kindled. How the earliest flame was kindled in Scotland, far out among the Atlantic rocks, in gusty Iona, "The Blessed Isle of the Dove (Columba)"—as the great French historian calls it,—I described in my first chapter. Like the vestal virgins of old, these earliest custodiers of the holy fire of Christ's blessed Evangel, felt that they dared not for their lives suffer it to go out. From hand to hand the sacred fire was passed: not as in the ancient games where the burning torch was passed from one runner to the other, and when he got it, the other lost it; but, as in the striking scene I have described,—the flame was passed from hand to hand; not, however, before each recipient had first kindled his own taper, he in turn becoming a centre of illumination for all the blackened torches around him,—until at last our little land became flooded with the light of Christianity, and bright with many a saintly star,—so bright indeed as to be remarkable throughout universal Christendom for its

> "Captains of the Saintly band,
> Lights who lighten every land,
> Princes who with Jesus dwell,
> Judges of His Israel!"

The great work of Christianizing Scotland and subjugating it to Jesus, and eventually enrolling it as a province of Christ's empire, was done by the disciples of St Columba—the Iona Missionaries. A central fact must here be noted and remembered—that St Columba and his followers for six hundred years had nothing whatever to do with Rome; they founded and established the National Church of this country, owning allegiance to no foreign potentate, but governed then as it is now by its own spiritual courts and officers. This is what may be called "The Culdee Period" (600-1100 c) the period in which the evangelisation of the country was conducted by the "Culdees" or missionary monks of Iona, all of whom were originally, like St Columba himself, of Irish extraction. They were called "Culdees" or "Celé Dé" or "Keledei,"—Gaelic words signifying "worshippers or servants of God." In course of time, wherever the Celtic language was spoken, the name was applied to anyone who, having laid aside the temporal cares of life, devoted himself to meditation and prayer. The original Culdees of Iona, who made the crooked places straight and the rough places plain, and Scotland Christian, were both monks and missionaries. They were ascetic in their habits, but, like the clergy of the Greek Church, were allowed to marry and to hold property. Sometimes they lived in solitary places, each, alone, a hermit life,—the original rule of their founder requiring each to live "in a fast place with one door." In St Serf's island, Loch Leven, there were very many of them, who lived in separate cells all over the little isle. But usually they formed themselves into a religious community, all living in one monastery, which was invariably dedicated to the Holy Trinity; and the number of the inmates was fixed at thirteen, in imitation of Christ and the Apostles—one abbot and twelve brethren. The original model of these Culdee houses was St Columba's apostolic college in Iona, and the aim of all his disciples was to reproduce in every district of Scotland a similar Christian community, which would be the centre of good influence to the heathen all around.

There has been a great discussion as to whether their church government was Episcopal or Presbyterian, and the subject has been hotly argued on both sides. In all probability, the Abbot of each Culdee establishment exercised Episcopal superintendence not only over his own monks, but over the whole district stretching for so many miles like a girth round their church. It is, however, quite an anachronism to project the modern bishop into Culdee times, for Church polity was then crude and unformed. The one aim of these men was not to elaborate a perfect system of Church government, but to gather in something to govern. All other questions were secondary to this,—how to bring entire Scotland in touch with the Cross. Towards the close of this period, the brethren of a community formally elected a bishop for themselves and their district, until the Crown, influenced by Rome, stepped in and deprived them of this privilege.

The day of a Culdee missionary opened and closed before the altar of heaven. The ancient ritual of Iona, which the Culdees clung to with loving tenacity, pretty much as England clung to the "Sarum use" for long after Rome had become dominant,—consisted of prayers, praise, and short extracts from the gospels: the Roman writers speak of their "barbarous rites" and "special use,"—pointing at the simplicity of their rites. Very probably the "Hymn of St Columba"—which the Celtic clergy loved so much, that they said their Master had it handed down to him from heaven, by one of the white-robed,—formed a frequent act in their common worship. It begins with praise of God and His works: it then describes the angelic world, the material creation, the stars and their motions, and then with a sublime beauty passes to the description of the future state—the glories of heaven, and the Paradise of God; concluding with an impressive picture of the Last Day,—which will bear some comparison with the "Dies Irae."

The worship done, and the solemn blessing over,—given by the grey haired abbot to the kneeling brethren,—the Culdee fathers sallied forth in twos to preach and teach the people around them. In misty moor, and gloomy Caledonian glen,—in the little Pictish towns, and by the shore of the restless sea,—these heralds of Christ were to be seen and heard. They were not unlike the old Druidical priests either in appearance or in their solitary manner of life: their hermit spirits roamed and dwelt apart. Their language would glow with Celtic fervour as they discoursed to the little circle of Picts gathered round them, of death, judgment, heaven, hell, God's power, and Christ's salvation. There is a very strong resemblance between Ossian's poetry and St Columba's hymn. Doubtless the same picturesque glowing imagery characterized their preaching. Strong in their convictions, brave in their endeavours, constant in their aim, unflinching in their self-denial,—they cared not to whom they spoke of Christ and the Cross. They preached even in the Court, and brought kings not only to worship at the feet of the King of kings, like the wise men of the East, but like them to offer gifts.

I can picture one of these old Culdee preachers describing the mystery of death to a group of awe-struck Highlanders—a mystery as mysterious to-day as ever,—and the hope of immortality, in language similar to that of the Icelandic ballad which was being sung far up in that more northern island—which they are known to have reached—at the very time when they were preaching in Caledonia:—

> " And now coiled up, with fevered blood,
> A grim old wolf I die,
> Whilst dripping skies above me spread
> And winds sob sadly by.
>
> O'er tiréd heart and drowsy head
> Does welcome slumber creep
> As little babe on mother's knee
> Will softly drop asleep.
>
> With folded feet and closed palms
> I will not stir nor wake,
> But hushed in happy dreaming lie
> Till the last morning break.

> And if men ask,—'who lieth thus?'
> Say,—' 'tis a tired breast
> Now finding peace,—finding calm,
> Finding rest!'"

Who knows but that, under their stern strong preaching, some Scottish Felix may have trembled. At anyrate, their preaching and example wrought a great change. All over the country, as if by magic, churches sprang up,—and even in secluded Highland glens the wild airs of the Celtic hymn awoke the echoes. Distinct traces of over sixty of their churches have been discovered. At St Andrews,—"The Canterbury of Scotland,"—they very early made a settlement. St Kainich, a contemporary of St Columba, had a cell there about 590. Very probably the St Rule or St Regulus who, according to the legend, arrived on the stormy shore of Fife from the East, with the relics of St Andrew the Apostle (from which circumstance the town got its name, and Scotland her patron saint and national symbol) was really St Riaghall, an Irish Culdee, who built a cell down near the shore, under the shadow of the present tall gaunt St Rule Tower, in the ancient archiepiscopal seat; and there

> "Good St Rule, his holy lay,
> From midnight to the dawn of day,
> Sang to the billows' sound!"

An ancient Scottish historian describes the Culdee missionaries going out from the old chapel of St Rule,—"the House of the Apostle on the brink of the wave,"—where the relics were kept,—and carrying the cross into the heart of heathen Scotland.

Another of their great centres was St Serf's island in beautiful mirror-like Lochleven, which was granted them in 842 by Brudo, King of the Picts. A very interesting relic remains of this great Culdee settlement,—namely, the catalogue of their monastic library, which consisted of a gradual, missal, and lectionary: "The Sentences of the Abbot of

Clairvaux:" "Three Books on the Sacrament:" Origen's works: Prosper's works: A Bible: The Acts of the Apostles: The Gospels: the three Books of Solomon: a commentary on Canticles: a Dictionary: a collection of "The Sentences:" an exposition of Genesis: and a book of ecclesiastical rules; a list of vestments is also included. The ruins of the little monastery are still standing on the wood-clad island, not far from which, on another island, once languished in compulsory seclusion, Scotland's fairest, but most unfortunate queen.

I can only mention the names of the other great Culdee settlements:—Aberdeen, Abernethy, Applecross, Arbirlot, Blair, Brechin—"given to the Lord for the Culdees" by Kenneth MacMalcolm; Cloveth, Deir—founded by St Drostan, a follower of St Columba; Dull—where the Father of Scottish Christianity once sojourned, and one of whose abbots in the eleventh century became the ancestor of a long line of Scottish kings; Dunblane, Dunfermline, Dunkeld, Ecclesgrig, Edzell, Falkirk, Glasgow, Glendochart, Govan, Hoddam—for eight years the see of St Mungo; Kettins, Kilgouerin, Kilmuir, Kilmund, Kilspindy, Kinneff, Kingarth in Bute, Kinghorn, Kirkmichael, Lesmahagow, Lismore—the see of Argyle for many years; Madderty, Melginch, Monifieth, Mortlach, Muthill, Old Dornoch, Old Montrose, Rosmarky, Rossin, Ratho, Selkirk, Scone—the great treasure of whose Abbey was "The Stone of Destiny," on which Jacob was said to have slept, and on which our sovereigns are crowned; Turriff. All these religious centres were founded by the Columban missionaries.

But so vast were their labours and so unwearied was their zeal, that they did not stop even with Scotland. The North of England was converted principally by these Scottish missioners, whom the English called by their Celtic name of "Culdees." A certain king of Northumbria, named Oswald, once sent to Iona for a missionary to convert his people to Christ. The Council of the Culdees at Iona met and selected St Aidan, one of their number, a man of singular gentleness, who journeyed to the south, and took up his seat at Lindisfarne, ever since called "Holy Isle" because of him, and which, from being the centre of Christian influence for Northern England, deserves the name of "the Iona of the East Coast."

Up till the middle of the eleventh century, we hear of Culdees serving in York Minster and still christianizing the South. Nay they spread to Wales and Ireland, even to Iceland, and out to the Continent, until in time, from Iona, the earliest metropolis of Scotland, pioneers of learning and religion went all over the west of Europe.

So famous did this Isle of Saints become, that one of the Popes—Pius V.—meditated a pilgrimage to it, in order that he might see the shrine from which so holy and powerful an influence had proceeded; and no less to see the celebrated "Crystal Book" of St Columba, which was said to have been given him by an angel; as well as a number of rare literary teasures, which, after the sack of Rome, were carried across sea and land to the island-cradle of Scottish Christianity. For six hundred years the eyes of Christendom were turned to this bright spot. So great was the traffic and so numerous were the pilgrims, that across the West Highlands a highway was marked out with pillared stones, the remains of some of which can still be traced across the Island of Mull, leading down to the stormy shore, from which the missionaries' coracle took the pilgrims across the green billowy Atlantic, out to the low streak of land from which the vaulted pile arose, beneath which so unique a piety was nourished.

So fragrant was the memory of the great Apostle of Scotland, that for several centuries the reapers in the island declared that ever and anon in the harvest field they caught a glimpse of his reverend presence, and felt a sweet perfume suffuse the sheaves which his hands had touched. It was his spirit that fired the Culdees, and it was the Culdees who made Scotland fit to be enrolled as a province in the world-wide Empire of Jesus Christ!

CHAPTER III.

UNDER THE SHADOW OF ST PETER'S.

Roman Period: 1100—1500.

IN the old church of Ruthwell, a few miles from Dumfries, there stands an enormous stone cross more than seventeen feet high, which has a history of almost unparalleled interest and charm. It is a richly-carved Runic cross, similar in appearance to those which are found in Iona and the West Highlands, and is all covered over with sculptures and writing. So strong had the Puritan influence from England grown in Scotland, about the middle of the seventeenth century, that the General Assembly of the Church ordered this cross, which from time immemorial had stood inside the church of Ruthwell, to be removed, as a monument of idolatry. The relic was ignominiously thrown down on its face, and left lying for about a hundred years on the pavement of the church; but in 1772 some zealous parishioners took "the accursed thing" out and threw it into the graveyard, where it was broken into several pieces, and where it lay for many long years, as neglected and forgotten as the ancestral graves which formed its resting-place. No one knew or cared to know what a priceless witness to the faith of Christ, whose distinctive emblem and crest it was,—an emblem of which no true Christian can ever feel ashamed,—lay covered up with rubbish and overgrown with grass in that neglected God's-Acre.

But in the year 1802, Dr Duncan, the enterprising and enlightened pastor of the parish, raised it up and pieced it together, and lately it has been re-erected in its pristine position inside the church, where it had stood before for nearly a thousand years. The deciphering of what has now become famous as "The Ruthwell Cross" is a marvellous story, and one of the greatest triumphs of scholarship in modern times. The stone is all covered with sculptures of Scripture scenes, most of them from the life of our Lord; but round the edge of the arms of the cross are long lines of inscription in Runic letters, and the interpretation of these has been at last arrived at in the following extraordinary manner. In the year 1823, a German scholar was making a literary pilgrimage through Northern Italy, and in the old conventual library of Vercelli he by accident came upon an ancient yellow parchment, on which, among other things, was written, in the Anglo-Saxon language, a short poem entitled "The Dream of the Holy Rood." He felt deeply interested in discovering this scrap of old English sacred minstrelsy in a land so far away, and in so unlikely a quarter; and after rendering it carefully into modern English, he saw to his infinite surprise that it was almost identical with the hypothetical translation of the Runic letters on the old stone in the Dumfriesshire church. After a great deal of elaborate research it has been finally settled that the Runic writing on the Ruthwell Cross is a copy of an ancient English poem, composed probably by Caedmon, and was carved about the year 665 A.D. Indeed, on the top of the cross the words are written—"Caedmon made me." It was therefore about the close of the seventh century of our Christian era that this religious poem—which seems to have been quite current and popular in England and the south of Scotland—was put into a more durable form on this stone cross. It is the "Story of the Cross" as told by a British Christian of the seventh century, in simple language, and with genuine feeling.

Here is the Ruthwell inscription put into modern English. The idea is that a Christian falls asleep, and sees the Cross, in a vision, surrounded by angels: and the Cross breaks forth into a soliloquy, and tells the story of what happened to it and to its Divine Bearer on the ever-memorable Crucifixion Day—the darkest day in history :—

"Twas many a year ago,
I yet remember it,
That I was hewn down
At the wood's end.
Then men bare me upon their shoulders
Until they set me down upon a hill.
Then saw I tremble
The whole extent of earth.
He mounted me;
I trembled when He embraced me;
Yet dared I not to bow earthwards.
I raised the powerful King
The Lord of the Heavens.
They pierced me with dark nails.
They reviled us both together.
I was all stained with Blood,
Poured from His Side.
The shadow went forth
Pale under the welkin.
All creation wept,
They mourned the fall of their King."

This is the "testimony of the rocks" to the Faith of Christ—a sermon in stone, preached twelve hundred years ago; but still its voice is heard proclaiming that faith wherein we stand, the faith of the Church of Scotland of to-day, as it was in that early Christian age. It is the same old gospel to-day as it was yesterday, and as it will be for ever.

Towards the middle of the eleventh century (about 1060) the Culdee Church, however, which was then about five hundred years old, showed unmistakable signs of decay and dissolution. Scottish Christianity seems to march in epochs of five hundred years:—five hundred years of heathen darkness; five hundred years of the Culdees; five hundred years of Rome; and now we are in the midst of another such cycle.

But the old enthusiasm of the first Iona missionaries had gone off, and the torch which they had lit showed signs of flickering; the Story of the Cross as told by them with so much zeal and fire to the heathen Picts, ceased to interest them. Their numbers fell off; their doctrines became loose and erroneons, and they ceased to perform their ministerial functions with vigour and effect. There was a *dead pause* in the history of Scottish Christianity in the last half of the tenth and the early years of the eleventh centuries; Christianity ceased to spread, and there was a danger of a lamentable relapse into heathenism. In many cases the monasteries were deserted, and the revenues which had accumulated in course of ages were used and enjoyed by laymen. At Dunblane (founded by the Culdee, St Blane), religion sank so low that the voices of devotion ceased altogether, save for one solitary chaplain who mumbled off a lifeless office in a roofless church.

And now, when the Scottish Church showed symptoms of failing health and vigour, *Rome* stepped in. The Church of Rome was then by far the most vigorous, as it was also the largest branch of Catholic Christendom, and as yet it was almost entirely free of those peculiar errors which afterwards disfigured it, and finally worked its doom. Its monastic orders were spreading all over Europe, and by their vigorous preaching and earnest lives of devoted self-denial, were bringing in the nations one by one to the obedience of the Church. And thus the "Shadow of St Peter's" stretched westwards and westwards, till, first the Gallican Church of France, which used to be distinct and independent of Rome, came under the Pope, and then the shadow crossed the narrow silver streak that separates our little rocky isle in the north-west of Europe from the great mainland, and first the Church of England, which for ages had been free and national and self-ruled, of which the thirty-seventh article of the English Church to-day was quite as true as it is now,—"that the Bishop of Rome hath no jurisdiction in this realm of England,"—was drawn in, and the Roman Ritual ousted the ancient Saxon characteristics; and then the shadow moved northwards, and covered Scotland, so that by the end of the twelfth century, almost every trace of the old Culdees had vanished, and the Church of Caledonia, like the Church of the South, had conformed to the law and order of what was really the strongest, the greatest, and the most missionary Church of mediæval ages: and the end of it was that all Europe, save Russia, Turkey, and Greece, lay under the shadow of St Peter's.

In the Acts of the Apostles it is related how, when St Peter walked abroad at eventide in Jerusalem, his shadow, as it fell on the sick and maimed in the streets of the Holy City, caused them to be healed. They even brought the sick out and laid them on couches in the streets and lanes, "so that at the least the shadow of Peter passing by might overshadow some of them." Whatever evil and deadly influence the shadow of that Church which claims to be founded on St Peter may have had in later times,—however true it may be that it became a *deadly night-shade,—* its influence at this time was all for good.

Wherever the shadow reached it left behind it enduring memorials of its presence. We are still surrounded by, and many of us worship every Sunday in, stately sanctuaries built by her hands; the present parishes of Scotland were all planned and mapped out by her: three out of the four Scottish Universities, and most of our great schools, were her creations: almost all our national institutions were of her invention: the very soil on which we live, and which is nourishing us to-day, was reclaimed by her assiduity from being a rocky dreary waste, covered over in many places with the impenetrable Caledonian Forest, into a rich agricultural possession: the monks of Newbattle were the first workers of coal in Scotland, and by developing the resources of the earth, became the fathers of Britain's industrial greatness: all over the country still there are remains of her wisdom, her energy, her unwearied and well-directed labours. "This land that was desolate is become as the garden of Eden." We dwell in that land which God gave to our fathers, and we have entered into their labours.

This was how the great ecclesiastical change from Culdeeism to Rome was effected. After the Norman Conquest of England (1066) thousands of Englishmen sought refuge in Scotland from the tyranny of William the Conqueror; and these brought with them across the Border, their customs, their rites, and in some cases their priests, who, like the whole of England, had become subject to Rome. But the proximate cause was the marriage of Malcolm Canmore, King of Scots, in 1070, to Margaret, the granddaughter of an English king. She too had been brought up in the English Church, and she became the great leavener of Scotland.

Her name signifies "a pearl,"—and a pearl she was, for her life, though spent in the luxury of the Royal Court of Scotland, never dimmed its saintly lustre; in the midst of her manifold queenly avocations, her pure and beautiful soul often stole away to Him who had bought it with His precious blood. Her heart was firmly fixed where true joys were alone to be found. In the midst of a beautiful country, of which she was the beloved sovereign, she sighed for a better country, that is an heavenly. Though wearing the crown of a land of heroes and patriots, Duncan and Macbeth, Ossian and Columba, she reached forth to the Crown that fadeth not away.

She built numberless churches and monasteries, and placed a useful and vigorous ministry in them, sweeping out the few weak and corrupt Culdee clergy that were left; she would not rest until she saw the laws of God and His Church observed throughout all her realm. She was devoted to her husband, and when on her dying bed she received news that he and her three sons were slain on the battlefield, she gave God thanks in these words:—"I thank Thee, O my God, that in this last period of my life, Thou makest my soul pass through terrible trials. But I hope they will serve to cleanse and refine it, and consume the dross of my sins. O, my Saviour Jesus, who by the will of my Father, and co-operation of the Holy Ghost, didst blot out my sins and deliver me from all evils, by Thy Sacred Body and Precious Blood, grant that I may adhere to Thy holy commandments, and never suffer me to be separated from Thee." And having whispered, "Lord Jesu, deliver me," she gently took her departure to the Bosom of Christ!

She was laid to rest in Dunfermline Abbey, which she herself had built in the place where her royal nuptials had been celebrated, and it was a great shrine for pilgrims for ages. Her dust was afterwards laid in the chapel in Edinburgh Castle, still called "St Margaret's Chapel," from which, it was said, there breathed out the fragrance of odorous spices and the flowers of spring. She was for several centuries regarded as the Patron and saintly Protectress of Scotland, as she undoubtedly was the Restorer of the Faith of Christ in our land. There is a legend that before the battle of Largs (1263) a poor crippled soldier saw her in a vision, with crowned head and stately steps, and followed by a train of the white-robed, going seawards to do battle for Scotland, her beloved fatherland; just as once, at Glastonbury in England, the monastery sacristan at dusk entertained two strangers in white, who, they declared, had to be off betimes in the morning, to strike for Scotland at Bannockburn. It was firmly believed long ago, that it was through St Margaret's influence that the Norse galleys were swept on to the fatal rocks, and that the land of the Thistle and the Heather, and the Burning Bush, remained free and unfettered as the waves that boom around its iron-bound coasts!

After her death, the work of establishing the Church was taken up with almost as much vigour by David I., well called by his successor in the throne, "the sair sanct for the Croun," because of the enormous sums which he spent from the royal exchequer in erecting bishoprics, and building and endowing cathedrals and monasteries. The whole country had been divided into parishes, the same as exist to-day, and in hundreds of cases the same old gray arching roof covers God's worshipping children as covered their ancestors in that dim and distant age of long ago.

But the greatest step of all was the division of Scotland into dioceses, over which a bishop or chief pastor was placed. St Andrews was founded by Queen Margaret about 1090, and in time it became the "Canterbury of Scotland," and the seat of the Archbishop of all Scotland north of the Forth. It is chronicled that its ritual and discipline and learning were unequalled all over the world. One of its earliest bishops was described on a stone slab which was raised near the high altar, as "a straight pillar of the Church, a bright window, a sweet censer and a melodious bell." Ever after 1329 the Archbishop of St Andrew's had the right of crowning the kings of Scotland on the old coronation-stone at Scone.

The See of Glasgow was established about the year 1100, and in time it became the seat of the Archbishop or Primate of all Scotland south of the Forth. The noble cathedral of St Mungo, as it now stands—"The Salisbury of Scotland"—though preceded by several stately churches, was built in 1225, with the proceeds of a collection made all over Scotland, in every church, by order of the Provincial Council. Vast sums came in from other countries: indeed it may be said that it was built with the offerings of universal Christendom. The Bishoprics of Galloway, Aberdeen, and Moray were founded by Queen Margaret about 1080-1090; Caithness in 1153; Brechin, Dunblane, Dunkeld, Dornoch, and Ross by King David, "the sair sanct," about 1150. For long the Orkney and Shetland isles were under the Norwegian Bishops, and were quite separate from ecclesiastical Scotland; their Cathedral was Christchurch in Bergen. Every new bishop on coming over from Norway was first put to the test of draining, at one draught, an ancient goblet, which was said to have belonged to St Magnus, the Orcadian patron. In 1471 these northern isles were joined to the Scottish Church and made into a Bishopric under the primacy of St Andrews.

It was not without a struggle, but in course of time the Roman Canon law and constitution became universal, and were found to work well. A great question, however, arose in the twelfth century as to the ecclesiastical authority to which the Church of Scotland was amenable. The Archbishop of York claimed to have jurisdiction over all Scotland, and asserted his right to consecrate the Scottish bishops. After a severe contest, in which the Scottish national feeling was more strongly intensified and consolidated than ever it had been before, and King, bishops, priests, and people all stood shoulder to shoulder, as one man, for their land and liberties, it was decreed by Rome that the Church of Scotland should be responsible to no ecclesiastical power whatever, but be directly subject to the Pope, and be his special child. The present occupant of the Papal chair (Pope Leo), in a recent famous pastoral, says : " The Roman Pontiffs took these sees under their especial protection, and treated them with special favour, and the Church of Scotland was the special daughter of the Apostolic See, and subject to no other." Hence, pilgrimages to Rome became very frequent on the part both of prelates and nobles,—as also to the Holy Sepulchre at Jerusalem. So that just as wise men came from the distant East to see where Christ was born, so devout men journeyed from the far West to see where He had been buried!

During all this age, we are told that preaching could not be heard for the sound of hammers and trowels, so great was the zeal and energy of the Church in rearing ecclesiastical edifices. The stately houses of God, which to-day are dotted all over this land of mountain and of flood, were largely the offspring of this age of wonderful activity and absolutely unparalleled generosity and self-sacrifice. God received the best of everything: the Church did not keep her alabaster box all to herself: she gladly broke it over the Redeemer's feet : and the House of God was filled with the odour of the ointment.

I have not space to speak of the *Monastic* system, which became so widespread, so powerful, and so useful. The white-robed Cistercian Monks were found at Melrose, Newbattle, Sweetheart, Culross, &c. ; the black-gowned Benedictines at Dunfermline, Arbroath (whose good-hearted abbot hung the renowned Inchcape bell to warn storm-tost mariners off the fatal rock), Coldingham, &c.; the Cluniacs at Paisley and Crossraguel; the Augustinians at Jedburgh, Holyrood, Cambuskenneth, Scoon. Hundreds of such religious houses were scattered over broad Scotland from lonely Kirkwall in the far north, to the yellow Solway shore; and they were for long centuries centres of learning and labour, of sweetness and light, both in spiritual and temporal affairs, homes of devotion and contemplation, calm refuges for human spirits wearied of the world.

These men combined both the pious and the practical: they were both Marthas and Marys, serpents and doves; their crest was not a mere bent knee but an uplifted hand as well. They looked well to their spiritual harvest, and yet neglected not the husbandry of the fields around them, which, even after the lapse of three centuries, are still rich and bountiful.

"It is good for us to be here," was the inscription written over the arched doorway of every Cistercian monastery, "where man lives more purely, falls more rarely, rises more quickly, treads more cautiously, rests more securely, dies more happily, is pardoned more easily, and rewarded more plenteously." It was by one of that same Cistercian order which colonised Melrose and so many other Southern abbeys, that the beautiful hymn (so great a favourite in the Church of Scotland to-day) was written, "Jesus, the very thought of Thee, with sweetness fills my breast." If you look up on one of the transept walls of Melrose Abbey, you will see an inscription, which embalms and embodies the same exalted sentiment and everlasting truth; carved up by some old monk of Melrose ages ago, it still stands, though worn and weather-beaten, in these words, "When Jesus *comes*, the shadow *goes!*" In the stately pile of St David's lying at the foot of the green swelling Eildon Hills, over which Thomas the Rhymer had roamed, the writer of that line may have watched the ever-changing lights and shadows sweeping across the hills on a summer day, with the sweet breath of the snow-wreathed hawthorn blossom coming in at his little groined window, and the thought occurred to him, that when Jesus, "the light of the world," shines into the soul, the shadows flee away, just like the fleeting patches of darkness on these rolling hills, as the day strengthens. Or it may have been at night, when the gloom was over mountain and valley, and the silvery Tweed rippled on in the darkness, singing its grand old eternal song of "men may come and men may go, but I flow on for ever," as it is doing just now as I write by its banks, when all at once the monastery bell rang out for the midnight office; and on that ancient altar, beneath which Bruce's heart lay buried, and before which many a Scottish king had thrown his soul at Christ's feet and begged succour for battle and Pilgrimage, the tapers slowly twinkled into flame, and the great dark echoing house of God was brightened with the kindly glow: so Christ, thought that solitary watcher, is the light of the world and of the soul. "O happy lights," was the language of his heart (the language of a great soul only lately removed from being an ornament in the same communion), as he knelt in adoration, making intercession for the silent world which lay asleep around him,—

> "O happy Lights, O happy Lights,
> Watching my Jesus livelong nights,
> How close you cluster round His throne,
> Dying so meekly, one by one,
> As each his faithful watch is done.
> Could I with you but take my turn
> And burn with Love of Him, and burn
> Till love had wasted me like you,
> Sweet Lights, what better could I do!"

For five hundred years the Church of Rome permeated with its institutions the whole of Scottish life; but towards the close of that period, what happened five centuries before to the Culdees, happened to Rome,—the shadow of St Peter's began to be a shadow of death and decay, and Scotland began to languish under it. Secondary doctrines of the Church were exaggerated into prime importance, and doctrines which had no right whatever to be there, and which Christ and the Apostles never sanctioned, took up the chief place in the Roman Theology, to the humiliation if not practical exclusion of Him who is the centre of Christianity, for Christianity is Christ and Christ only. The Church had built its tabernacles—and beautiful tabernacles they were—on the hill of vision, but it began to look at Moses and Elias and the poor human followers of the Saviour, rather than at "Jesus only!" And so it happened to them,—as it will always happen under similar circumstances, in whatever church and age it may be,—that the old Melrose inscription was reversed, "Jesus *went*, and the shadow *came!*"

CHAPTER IV.

THE DECLINE AND FALL OF ROME.

1500—1560.

In the year 1559 Queen Elizabeth passed a statute requiring clergymen who had a difficulty in reading, to con over their Scripture lessons carefully beforehand. It is a striking illustration of the crass ignorance of the Church in that age. To know Greek in the last half of the fifteenth and first half of the sixteenth centuries, was to be a suspected person; to know Hebrew was to be a heretic. The plurality of worlds was proved by the text, "Were there not ten made, but where are the nine?"—the flatness of the earth by the passage, "He stretcheth out the heavens as a curtain," the prevalent idea being, that the world was a ship, sailing majestically through space, with sun, moon, and stars gleaming like lights at the masthead, and the deep blue sky for a sail! The Church has imprisoned and burned several who declared the opposite.

Very few even of the prelates and kings could sign their names, and had to content themselves with scrawling a dirty cross on the vellum, sometimes the scribe adding the explanatory observation, "The sign of the cross (+) in his own hand, on account of his ignorance of letters." Very probably the practice of Roman prelates prefixing a cross to their signatures, as is still their wont, is a relic of the time when that sign was all they could write, just as the practice of "reading the line" before singing the psalm was, in later days, on account of the people being unable to read.

In early ages, the monasteries had not only been homes

of devotion, but seats of learning, where alongside of the Golden Candlestick of God, the lamp of scholarship burned peacefully in the midst of gross barbarism and bloody battles; but in this age it was despised. Even a Pope declared that he was above grammar; as the satirist put it, the priests and monks began to prefer lamb to languages, bags to books, salmon to Solomon, Martha to Mary.

Throughout the land generally a spirit of worldliness had crept in, and would not go out. There had been a time when the Church was the minister of the poor and downtrodden. On one occasion, the monks of Melrose, during a great famine, fed four thousand starving wretches who came and knocked piteously at the monastery gates, and who for three months lived in little huts or booths reared on the slopes of the Eildon Hills and in the greenwood that fringes the broad-bosomed Tweed, enjoying the benevolence of those true, self-denying servants of Christ, until the yellow corn was ready for the glittering sickle. How different it was in the closing years of the fifteenth century; these same monks of Melrose who had ministered to others, and whose motto had been, "In all things let God be glorified," now

"drank good ale
On Fridays when they fasted;
They never wanted beef nor kail
So long as *their neighbours'* lasted."

One of the arches of that Abbey, which was practically rebuilt in 1544, is supported by the figure of a monk who writhes in the grip of an evil Spirit; it is a type of what was really taking place at that very time. Another carving represents a monk holding in one hand a string of prayer-beads, which he counts, and with the other pulling out his ear so as to hear better the voice of some tempting worldly charmer. There is the secret of that ruined pile! They were rich and increased with goods, and had lack of nothing: and so they fell spiritually asleep, and the lamps, both of religion and learning, went out; and, at midnight, the Bridegroom came!

Even Roman writers and historians themselves acknowledge the tremendous corruption of all the ministerial orders in the closing years of the fifteenth and first half of the sixteenth centuries. Archdeacon Bellenden of Aberdeen, shortly before the crash came, went the length even of saying that it would have been well if St David had not endowed the monasteries so richly, for these riches had proved a snare to evil-minded prelates who "raged in most insolent and corrupt life," and who had made the Church of God "ane sicker net to draw all manner of gold and silver out of this realm to Rome!"

The religious houses were not all thus, it is true. James V. was urged by one of his court-advisers to demolish the monasteries, as greedy, dissolute Henry VIII. had done, who loved the Reformers only because he hoped they would palliate his lusts and condone his robberies; but "God forbid," said the more pious Scottish King, "God forbid that I should remove the *land-marks of God:* if a few be not good, should all the rest be destroyed? Though some be not, there be a great many good: and the *good may be suffered, and the evil may be reformed!*"

It was a noble speech and it was nobly acted on, for he set himself manfully to the work of cleansing the Temple and of scourging out corruptions in high places. He saw the thunder-cloud on the horizon, and heard with apprehension the first ominous rattle of the approaching storm: and so he not only tried like Abraham to count up as many worthy souls as would save the city, but he strove actually to increase their number.

The Scottish Parliament in 1540 declared that "the negligence of divine service, the dishonesty and misrule of kirkmen both in wit, knowledge, and manners, is the chief cause why kirk and kirkmen are made light of and contemned. For remedy whereof the king's grace exhorts and prays all archbishops, ordinaries, and other prelates, and every churchman in his own degree, to reform themselves, their obedientiaries and churchmen under them, in habit and manners to God and man."

In 1549 an ecclesiastical Council held in Edinburgh echoed these very sentiments. Two years before the Reformation, 1558, the great Council of Edinburgh made a last dying effort to reform the ancient organisation, but mortification had set in. It was a case of Laöcoon struggling with the snake. Even bishops and archbishops were known to lead immoral lives, and their coats of arms were sometimes quartered with the heraldic devices of their unlawful loves. The system of enforced celibacy resulted in open profligacy! The cord was pulled too tightly and it snapped, and those who pulled and in whose hands it snapped, would not set themselves to mend it; forgetting that when the silver cord of morality was loosed, the golden bowl of God's Candlestick would very soon necessarily be broken!

> "The air of Paradise should fan the House,
> And angels office all!"

That was the original idea of the Christian Temple and its ministry; but the atmosphere became worldly and polluted, and the angels' wings were clipped! The public as a body are difficult to move, one way or another; if not their strength, at any rate their preference, is to sit still. And corruptions must have reached a deplorable length, when the Scottish people, religious almost to superstition ("all you Scotch are superstitious," is the character England gives us), could not only look on complacently and see their ancient heritage razed, but actually lend a vigorous hand in the work of demolition, the prime movers of the "Reformation" being actually some half dozen of the Roman priests themselves, chief among whom was John Knox. It was not a Reformation from without but from within, instigated and carried out by men who had been within the inmost circle of Church life, and, breathing its atmosphere, were at last driven out by its stifling closeness and impurity.

At the Reformation, the Church owned about a third of the whole of Scotland. All important State offices were held by prelates. There was no harm in this had the influence been a good and a pure and a really Christian one, but while with one hand they seemed to reach out to heaven, with the other they groped about for the black hand of Evil, and took a very firm grip of the good things of this world.

Besides the ignorance and moral irregularities of the clergy, there were several other potent causes which brought about the great religious change of 1560. The Church exacted from the people a number of grievous and galling dues. When a person died, the vicar of the parish had the right of appropriating the best cow which was in the possession of the deceased, called therefore the "Kirk cow;" as well as the uppermost or "Upmaist cloth" on the bed of the dead man, or the best of his clothes, as a recompence for the funeral and the deliverance of the soul from purgatory. The Pasche or Easter offerings, the teind-ale and other ecclesiastical taxes, "the accustomed dues," were not only levied, but levied in such a way that the beneficiaries came to be thoroughly hated and despised; so much so that in the year before the great crash, a council decreed that "for avoiding popular murmur" the Easter and other taxes should be repealed.

In addition to this, ecclesiastical law and discipline were weakly and unjustly administered. Not only was an inefficient and immoral ministry winked at by those who differed from them only in this, that they were their judges, though both were equally sinners against the same laws, but the pernicious practice came in vogue of vacant incumbencies, abbacies, priories, and bishoprics being filled up by laymen, who merely wanted to draw the emoluments; or else the office was given temporarily (*sic*) in trust ("in commendam") to some nobleman or gentleman, or even to an infant in arms, until it suited the patron to appoint a permanent ecclesiastic. The *living* was the end, not the *charge;* the shepherd's *purse* had stronger attractions than the shepherd's *crook!* A few years before the Reformation, Paisley and Dunfermline Abbeys were ruled by secular persons, and not by monks at all; noblemen usurped many of the richest ecclesiastical livings, and gave no spiritual services in return, and thus the House of God was desecrated, and unholy fire was offered by these Korahs, at the altars of Heaven.

The deep-seated cause of the decline and fall of the Roman Church in Scotland, as elsewhere, was, however, that latterly it had failed to hold up before the people the Religion and Person of Christ in their purity, clearness, fulness, and simplicity. Theology was neglected in the monasteries and colleges; the Bible was almost forgotten, and very often never read even in church—indeed, sometimes the "Ethics" of Aristotle or some other good books were read aloud instead of those Eternal Words of Life from that Sacred Page through whose letters there shine the glories of another land.

Preaching was despised; the services of the Church were conducted in a dead language, which was unintelligible to the people and to most of the clergy; the common people had no catechisms or hymn-books by which they might be familiarised with the eternal facts and verities of Christianity. Just on the eve of the Reformation, Archbishop Hamilton of St Andrews published a catechism in the vulgar tongue, for the use of the clergy and people generally, in which the great Catholic truths of Christianity were plainly set forth, but it was too late, for the neglect of true catholic teaching had been of too long standing, and the enemy was thundering at the gates. Even after the invention of printing, and when it would have been possible and easy to do so, the Church did not circulate God's Holy Word, and checked the action of those who would have done what was its own proper and highest work. It failed as a religious educator, and the masses were growing up under the impression that Christianity consisted in a certain number of observances and acts, while the nature of God Almighty, the life and character of God's Son, the work and power of God's Spirit, the grand mission of God's Church to bring the nations to the foot of the Cross, were all passed by. More attention was paid to the arm-bone of St Giles than to the outstretched arms of Jesus on the Cross: a visit to Restalrig Chapel at the foot of Arthur's Seat, where diseases of the eye were cured, was of more importance than a visit to Calvary, where the disease of the soul had its remedy. A pilgrimage to the lonely treeless Isle of May, with its basaltic cliffs, away out in the swell of the German Sea, was sure to prove a blessing to women, and an hour spent before the shrine of Scone was but the beginning of good fortune. These paltry shrines were reverenced, and Bethlehem and Golgotha forgotten. A huge crowd of rites and ceremonies covered up the foundation-truths of Christianity which the Church still possessed, but hid in a napkin in the earth. They tithed mint and anise and cummin, and neglected the weightier matters of the law. And so the multitude of secondary and erroneous doctrines and practices covered up the great Catholic truths of the Church of God.

Stretching for three miles along the shore of the Moray Firth, near Forres, lie the Culbin Sands. They have a strange history. They cover up what was once a very fruitful pasture, where stood a stately manor-house, and lay rich farms. One night of awful storm in 1676, a mighty sand-wreath swept up and buried the whole estate, which ever since has been lost, and which to-day lies a long dreary stretch of yellow waste. Culbin is a type of what the Roman Church in Scotland had become at this stage of its history. Still the great Christian verities lying at its foundation, but buried! The soul of the country cried out for God, even the living God, and the Church gave the hungry soul a stone. Man cannot be happy, and society cannot prosper without a glimpse of the unseen, for the make of man's soul is immortal: and so they cried, "Clear away these sands which ages have accumulated, and let us get at the Rock of Ages!"

Not content, however, with proving a spiritual dead-weight to the country, it persecuted those who desired to see things better, and who wished no ill to their Spiritual Mother, the Church, and who, in point of fact, never left it, till they saw that the Ship in which they had been trying to weather the storm was sure to founder. Thomas Forrest, Dean of Dollar, Patrick Hamilton, a youth of royal blood, David Straiton, Alexander Kennedy, George Wishart, Walter Mill, and others, were all burned at the stake for claiming the liberty of reading and preaching God's Word. When any Church, Catholic or Protestant, resorts to persecution, its days are numbered : for the stake and the faggot and the pillory are the last resorts of a crumbling cause. Truth needs fire to purify it, but not to preserve it.

The modern spirit which had awakened in Europe at the Renaissance was abroad, and the world was beginning to wake up intellectually from the sleep of ages and to rub its eyes. There was with this spirit of inquiry mingled to some extent a spirit of revolution and of defiance of all restraints. A new development of Christianity was about to take place, and the birth was not without much pain and travail. Revolutionists wanted to abolish all law in the universal upheaval; the Scottish nobles taken as a whole, though professing at first great zeal for the Reformed Faith, showed by their subsequent conduct that all they really cared for was to have a good share of the Church's patrimony—the loaves and fishes,—for as soon as they had got all the Church lands on which they could lay their greedy fingers, they almost all forsook the Church, and fled and formed a religious sect for themselves. But the great mass of the Scottish people wanted neither Revolution nor infidelity nor injustice, but only a more real and truly Christian Faith ; their aspiration was that out of the ashes of the old Phœnix, whose wings had overshadowed Scotland for so many centuries, there might arise another and a fairer creation.

There were thousands of the Scottish clergy, monks, and people, who sighed for better, brighter days, and a nobler life, and who, perhaps, in the very words, at any rate in the same spirit, offered with deep fervency the touching prayer with which that Sovereign, in whose reign these mighty forces and influences came to a head, the beautiful Mary, Queen of Scots, went to the scaffold:—

> " O Lord God, Most High,
> I have trusted in Thee;
> O come, dearest Jesus,
> Now liberate me!
> Bound with a chain
> In terrible pain
> I still yearn for Thee!
> In sorrow I languish,
> I bend down in anguish,
> And adore, and implore Thee
> To *liberate* me!"

CHAPTER V.

A NEW PHŒNIX ARISES OUT OF THE ASHES OF THE OLD.

The Reformation: 1560.

SEATED amongst the beautiful ruins of Lincluden Church near Dumfries,—"sweet Lincluden's holy cells,"—Robert Burns wrote the following lines, addressed to that ancient shrine :—

> " Ye holy walls that, still sublime,
> Resist the crumbling touch of Time,
> How strongly still your form displays
> The Piety of ancient days !
> As through your ruins hoar and grey,
> Ruins, yet beauteous in decay,
> The silvery moonbeams fly :
> The forms of ages long gone by
> Crowd thick on Fancy's wandering eye,
> And wake the soul to musings high.
> E'en now as lost in thought profound
> I view the solemn scene around
> And pensive gaze, with wistful eyes,—
> The Past returns,—the Present flies ;
> Again the dome in pristine pride
> Lifts high its roof and arches wide,
> That, knit with curious tracery,
> Each Gothic ornament display,
> The high-arched windows painted fair
> Show many a saint and martyr there ! "

There are very few reasonable Scotsmen now-a-days who do not share and echo our great national bard's feelings of sorrow at the wide-spread demolition of the ancient sanctuaries of our Fatherland. As a Scottish patriot and Christian (in a far higher and truer sense than many of his more sanctimonious and censorious contemporaries, for the man who could not read that chapter in the Apocalypse which speaks so touchingly of "God wiping away all tears from the eyes," without visible emotion, as Burns could not, was no enemy to Christ and goodness) he deplored that fanaticism and bigotry which ruined that pile and nearly wrecked his own life.

The ruined houses of God which bestrew our land strike foreigners at once, who cannot believe that it was the White Hand of religion that tore down these stately Homes of Piety, but the Red Hand of some disastrous war. How far they are right, and others who ought to know better are wrong, I hope to show before I am done.

Nathaniel Hawthorne in his "Note-books" speaks of the "everlasting chill and damp of Glasgow Cathedral," and of the neglect of the wonderful crypt, whose marshalled arches and piers strike everyone with awe; and then of the charge of twopence for admittance which he archly refers to. St Giles' Cathedral he describes as having been "kirkified into three divisions by the Covenanters," and Greyfriars (Stirling) and Linlithgow as "uglified with pews and galleries and white-wash." Lockhart, Scott's biographer, is in his element when lashing the Reformers for their treatment of the churches, abbeys, and cathedrals. Glasgow Cathedral "is one of very few which have escaped from the demolishing fury of the first disciples of John Knox," and he speaks sarcastically of "The Dripping Aisle" there, so-called because of the damp and water which ooze through the crannies of the crazy roof. "Such was the perfection of their barbarity," he says, speaking of Melrose Abbey, "that they sprung new arches,—deforming with their sacrilegious intrusion,—memorable trophies of the triumph of self-complacent ignorance : but the Presbyterians have now removed from the precincts of the old sanctuary, and the miserable little kirk they have erected at the distance of a few fields, does not disturb the impression of its awful beauty."

The poet Southey was shocked when he first saw Melrose Abbey,—"the middle of the church converted into a kirk, this abominable den of sacrilegious Calvinism." "Come," exclaimed Dr Samuel Johnson to Principal Robertson, as he was being taken over the three kirks of St Giles, "let me see what was once a church!" And the ruins of Elgin Cathedral were to him a proof of "the waste of the Reformation," "and the intolerable violence of the Reforming ruffians." Looking on the Western Isles, he said: "The malignant influence of Calvinism has blasted ceremony and decency together; and if the remembrance of papal superstition is obliterated, the monuments of papal piety are likewise effaced!" "Yes, my lord," cried the Dunblane worthy to Archbishop Laud, as he rode past the old Cathedral with its famous oval west window praised by Ruskin, "before the Reformation it was a brave kirk!" "What, fellow?" said Laud, as he looked at the roofless nave, "*Deformation*, not *Reformation!*"

One could cite similar sentiments by the score, if it were necessary; but indeed there are very few now-a-days who do not share the sorrow expressed in them, however different the historical philosophy may be which accounts for existing appearances. Between Archbishop Laud, mourning over the ruins of Dunblane, and Canon Liddon in our own day, sitting, Marius-like, amongst the ecclesiastical wreck of St Andrews, there is a great army of sympathisers and witnesses, who, like Jeremiah, stand behind the crumbling wall of many a fair Scottish Abbey and make it a Christian wailing-place.

And no wonder; for no country has suffered in this respect as Scotland has done: but in your sorrow be just! A child when it is angry will throw its book or its spoon even at the head of its mother, if she should seem to side with the little one's offender. The act is instigated by anger, not by judgment and sweet reasonableness. And nothing is easier than for you in this comfortable, easy-going nineteenth century, to take up your little stool, and throw it, across three centuries, at the devoted head of John Knox, and ban him as the author and finisher of the destruction of ancient Scottish Christianity with all its monuments and beauties. An angry person must have someone or something to hit: it is a relief to the feelings of fallen man. John Knox has been made the ecclesiastical target for many a long day, and it is a target which has been well practised on. What between Catholics and Protestants, the figurehead of the Scottish Reformation has been pretty well defaced, and after coming through it all, this stern priest who shook Scotland to its foundations, may, like the apostle, give "thanks that I am what I am!" The old rhyme which the Catholic priest wrote upon him is not stronger than the language often heard to-day:—

> "That false apostate priest,
> Enemie to Christ and man's Salvation,
> Your maister Knoxe!"

I pass now from fancies to facts: there were two sides to the great Reformation movement as initiated and carried out in Scotland by John Knox—Destruction and Construction — the burning of the old Phœnix and the Resurrection of the new!

Was Knox really the author of these sacred ruins which lie scattered all over our land, by gentle river-side, amid fair woodlands, on the bleak sea-shore and the ocean-washed island? Certainly not! Most of the southern abbeys—Melrose, Kelso, Dryburgh, Jedburgh, Coldingham, Eccles, Dunbar, Haddington, Newbattle, Leith, Holyrood—were destroyed and burned by English armies. The marks of English fire can still be traced in blackened walls and cracked gables. There was no wanton pillage recommended or sanctioned by the first Reformers. They, as Catholic priests, venerated the ancient religious homes of Scotland, whose very dust to them was dear. All they wanted was to see the tawdry finery and superstitious trash swept out, and the noble abbeys and cathedrals left, still adorned with the Beauty of Holiness; and Religion still the sister and ally of Art.

It is a vile calumny on Knox to say that he instigated the pulling down of churches—as vile as to say that because the Dominican monks of Milan cut through Leonardo da Vinci's celebrated fresco of "The Last Supper," and mangled the figure of the Saviour, in order to make the door of their dining-room bigger, which alas! they did, that, therefore, the Church of Rome hated Art. It is a trite historical fact that Knox went out in person to save the monastery of Scone from the violence of "the rascal multitude." There is no real evidence that he said, "Pull down the nests, and the rooks will not return," although the charge has been shrieked in every note of the vituperative gamut! In some cases damage was done, but it was because great provocation was given. "The Reformation," wrote Knox, "is somewhat violent because the adversaries be stubborn!"

The Reformers had a vast multitude of camp-followers who simply wanted to make capital out of the universal havoc. The nobles, long jealous of the Church, gladly helped to rifle the rich monasteries and became "Commendators" of the lands, that is, *took care of them!* I do not think history can produce such another wonderful example of *affectionate care*. In times of keen excitement, a populace will always go too far, and they did, though Knox restrained them.

Special laws were passed by the Reformed Church of Scotland in 1560 at its first Assembly, providing that "no injury be done to glass or ironwork in churches, and that the cathedrals and minsters if used for divine service should be carefully maintained." The "First Book of Discipline," written by Knox, which is a summary of directions for the conduct of the Church's work under the new conditions, is very stringent in requiring that the churches be kept in good state, "lest that the word of God and the ministration of the sacraments, by *unseemliness of the place*, come into contempt," and that they should have "such preparation within as appertaineth as well to the *majesty of the Word of God*, as unto the ease and commodity of the people," and that "every church be furnished with a bell, a pulpit, a basin for baptizing, and a table for the celebration of the Holy Eucharist."

Over and over again we read in the Acts of early General Assemblies of the Church, complaints of the ruinous and unseemly state of many of the churches; and even Melville in 1584 declares that "by the insatiable sacrilegious avarice of earls, lords, and gentlemen, the kirks lie like sheep and cattle folds, rather than places for Christian congregations to assemble in!" All that Knox and the Reformers wanted, was that the old Church of Scotland should be cleansed of superstitions and abuses, of which everyone was heartily sick, and none more so than the clergy themselves, for they took the initiative in the work of reform.

There was nothing in the doctrine or principles of the Reformed Church to sanction or countenance the destruction of what was true, beautiful, and good in Roman Christianity; they wanted all the good and eternal elements carried on and ennobled; and as a matter of fact, the destruction and waste of churches and sacred furnishings, and the subsequent bareness and baldness of our Scottish sanctuaries and ritual, were directly in the teeth of Knox's teaching and preaching, and were due to the following causes, viz.,—the ravaging English armies; the utter selfishness of the nobles and gentry, who only wanted the Church's gold, and cared not a rush for the Church's doctrine, and who when called upon and *forced, as Knox had to force them with iron hand*, to make a decent provision for the Church and Holy Ministry, tried to get off as cheaply as possible, building miserably plain churches, something between a barn and a sepulchre—true "Heritors' Gothic," and giving back to the parson a mere trifling percentage of the rich funds which they had appropriated, but which were still by rights the Church's dower, evidently under the impression that "a poor church was a pure church," and that when the ministry could say with St Peter, "Silver and gold have I none," it would then, like St Peter, work miracles; the ignorant zeal of the Protestant mob, disgusted with clergy who, like the last vicar of Tongland, was an Italian mountebank, and could amuse the Court by his tight-rope feats at Stirling Castle; and last, but not least, the Puritan influence of later days, especially in Cromwell's time, which, coming from England, swept out of the Church of Scotland all her grand old Reformation traditions, together with her liturgy, ritual, polity, and spirit. It was in 1649 that a beautiful piece of carved marble in Aberdeen Cathedral, a piece of the finest altar carving in the world, with beautiful white angels and rich tracery, was ruthlessly smashed by the hand of the minister himself, acting under the spell of English Puritanism. The Church of Scotland owes the bald worship of an age now nearly past, and the ugly ecclesiastical architecture out of which she is so rapidly growing, *not to Knox or any Scotsman whatever, but to the English Puritans;* and if the Church of Scotland to-day is improving her worship and making the house of God more worthy of Him who dwells in the Burning Bush, and thus "imitates England," as is so often said, our reply is, England may very well give us back a little of that of which her Puritan preachers robbed us and our ancient Church two centuries ago. But we do not, and we do not wish, to "imitate England;" ours is the *National Scottish Church;* and these are not *innovations*, but *restorations* of the Spirit and worship and doctrine of the early Reformed Church!

In addition to requiring that God's house should be comely, and beautiful, and dignified, Knox arranged for the celebration of a reverent ritual, the preaching of true Catholic doctrine, and the continuance of the regularly-ordained orders of clergy. He set over the Church "*Superintendents*," or bishops to rule the pastors of the land, all of whom were, however, subject to the General Assembly. Knox was himself offered an English bishopric,

A NEW PHŒNIX ARISES OUT OF THE ASHES OF THE OLD. 55

and was on terms of the closest intimacy with the ecclesiastical dignitaries of the great sister church, his two sons in time becoming clergymen in the Church of England. The two national churches entered into a very near and close relationship.

The "orders of the clergy of the Church of Scotland" to-day are as truly valid, and in the Apostolic Succession, as the orders of any other Branch of the Church Catholic. All our ministers have received ordination from these half-dozen Reformers, who had themselves been duly ordained priests in the old church. So that there is no break in the succession from St Columba to the present hour, in that solemn "laying on of hands," which is commanded in the sacred Scriptures.

In 1557 the Protestant Lords of Scotland resolved that the English Book of Common Prayer should be regularly used in churches, and that it be the law and guide of the Scottish Church. But in 1560, John Knox prepared the prayer-book of the Church of Scotland, "The Book of Common Order," which was commanded by the General Assembly to be used, and which was Scotland's public service-book for more than two generations. Many people imagine that the Scottish Church has no prayer-book, and is at the mercy of any stray preaching presbyter, and his unchastised effusions. This is a grievous mistake. Beautiful prayers they are which Knox prepared for Scotland, and which were regularly read, with some short space for brief extempore petitions, like the "Bidding prayer" in the English Church, till the English Puritans got the Church of Scotland to say at the Westminster Assembly that it would part with its ancient ritual for the sake of uniformity.

In this "Book of Order" all the offices of the church are carefully explained and unfolded. The order for the "celebration of the Holy Communion" is exceedingly beautiful; the old Scottish custom was to celebrate once a month at five in the morning, as is still the custom in Holland. Daily service was enjoined in all town churches, and in the country occasionally during the week : all marriages were performed in church, a practice which was strictly adhered to down to the year 1700, when marriages in private houses became fashionable among the rich, who could enjoy the privilege by paying an ecclesiastical fine. At funerals there were generally a short homily on death, a prayer and a funeral hymn in the house, and always service at the grave. At the ordinary Sunday services, the people always repeated " Amen " at the end of each prayer, and said the Apostles' Creed and Lord's Prayer aloud with the minister. The congregation always knelt at prayer and rose to praise ; the minister was often assisted by a reader. A few hymns were sung as well as the psalms and scripture canticles. Churches were always dedicated to the memory of Testament saints. Fasting was strictly enjoined, and special days of entire abstinence from food were commanded by Knox. The chief commemorations of the Christian year—Christmas, Easter, Pentecost—seem to have been kept as in every other Reformed Church without exception.

Such was the constructive part of Knox's work : he first threw down and then built up; the old phœnix of Roman Christianity was burned, and out of its ashes sprang the new church, which was after all just the old Scottish Church in a new dress. " Where was your Church before the Reformation?" was the famous question addressed by a Roman Catholic to a distinguished Protestant ; and the answer is as famous as it is forcible, " Where was your face before it was washed ?"

CHAPTER VI.

A SCOTTISH HILDEBRAND.

Andrew Melville and the Rise of Presbyterianism:
1572—1603.

"GERMANY is not going back to Canossa," said Prince Bismarck in the German Parliament more than a dozen years ago. The remark, which has now become proverbial, recalls a strange scene in European history. Pope Gregory VII. or Hildebrand, a blacksmith's son, fell foul of the German Emperor, Henry IV., in regard to the rights of the Crown to appoint priests to benefices, and the shameless simony of which the bishops and other dignitaries, appointed by the Emperor, had been guilty. Hildebrand, who had been a monk at Cluny, mounted the steps of the Papal chair, determined to re-establish discipline throughout the Christian world; and so he set his face against the irregular morality of so many of the priests, put a firm foot down on simoniacal practices, and the custom of receiving investiture to sacred offices from lay hands. He exhorted the pastors of the Catholic world to lay down their lives rather than betray the laws of God to the will of man, even though that man should wear purple round his shoulders and gold round his brow.

The German Emperor seems to have cared very little either for religion or morality, only for a well-filled treasury and victorious battle-fields. To effect the former end he oppressed the Church within his dominions, robbed her of her revenues, and, on his own responsibility, made important ecclesiastical appointments: in a word, he trod the Church under foot, and ended a long course of rebellious pride and vaulting ambition, by pretending to depose the Pope.

At last, driven to desperation, Hildebrand put Germany under the Papal ban, and the voices of devotion ceased to be heard murmuring round the altars of the land; and the sweet church bells were hushed in town and hamlet, and a deep death-like shadow and gloom rested over the Fatherland. One after another the prelates and princes gave in, and expressed their sorrow, and united to elect a new emperor, and to banish the monarch whose pride had led them all so grievously astray.

And then Henry—poor, weak-minded coward that he was—finding he had gone too far, offered the Pope that he would undergo any humiliation to have the ban unsaid, the curse removed, and himself re-instated in the throne of his ancestors, with the blessing of the Church. After some hesitation Hildebrand accepted these terms.

It was on a cold winter day—the 25th of January 1077—that a knock came to the massive gates of Canossa Castle, in Northern Italy, where the Pope was staying on a visit. There was deep snow on the ground, and the white blinding drift went swirling and howling round the great old mediæval keep. It was a king who knocked at the door, naked, save for a piece of sackcloth round his body, barefooted, and discrowned, a miserable penitent, ashen-pale with fasting. For three days the Pope let him wait out in the Castle courtyard, and refused to see the rebellious Prince. And on the evening of January 27th—a memorable day for the Teutonic race—the suppliant Emperor was brought in, nearly dead with fatigue and exposure, and on his knees begged forgiveness for himself and his people—a request which was granted on the one condition, that he did not resume the Iron Crown till his case had been examined and finally decided. It is one of the most remarkable scenes in European history—Germany in the person of its Sovereign, doing penance at the feet of the Church. And the name of "Hildebrand" has gone forth to all time as the generic designation for an unbending, unflinching ecclesiasticism, and a high exclusive spiritual autocracy!

Scotland has had a Hildebrand in her history—one who set God's laws above all earthly laws, governors, and governments—who enthroned King Jesus above all kings, and whose motto really was, "The Church has spoken, and therefore it is!" Extremes meet very often and very strangely in life and history. Hildebrand was a Roman Catholic, Andrew Melville was a Presbyterian, and yet to all intents and purposes the two men are identical—both extreme High Churchmen—exclusive spiritual aristocrats, the one a Pope under cloth of gold, the other a Pope under a Geneva gown!

John Knox died in 1572, having breathed out with his last breath the Lord's Prayer, the Creed, and some hymns and sentences. He pointed upwards with his dying hand, and fell back upon his pillow, and so his soul passed into the Great Lone Land! "There lies one who never feared the face of mortal man," was the panegyric spoken by the Regent Morton over his grave, under the shadow of the old fretted crown of St Giles' Cathedral, where he had so often ministered.

The Church of Scotland, as reformed by Knox in 1560, continued to progress satisfactorily till about 1572, when a great controversy began. Now that all the old Roman Bishops and Abbots were removed or reformed, what was to become of the lands and benefices which, according to law, only they or such as they could hold or enjoy? The nobility wept with joy as they thought of the glorious work of reformation to which they had pledged themselves, but their tears were pretty much crocodiles' tears for the tempting, tasty temporalities which they saw being borne down in their direction, on the tumultuous river of political and religious change. To prevent the lands and revenues of the old Church passing out of the hands of the Reformed Church of Scotland, the *Convention of Leith* in 1572—a great gathering of superintendents and ministers—passed a resolution that the old titles of "archbishop," "bishop," &c., should be retained, and that through these ecclesiastical channels the ecclesiastical properties should be retained by the General Assembly.

The General Assembly which met in Perth in August 1572, concurred generally in this arrangement. But these new bishops, who were only to be the *agents for drawing funds which would otherwise have been lost*, did not command much respect. The people called them "Tulchan-bishops," the old Scotch "tulchan" being a stuffed calf which was supposed to make the cow give milk liberally. Like the good old Quaker to his ambitious offspring, they asked the new prelates, "My son, thee thinks thee has a *call to preach ;* but hast thou also considered well whether the people have a *call to hear thee ?*"

Andrew Melville had just returned to Scotland from Geneva, where he had studied under Beza and Calvin : and seeing the state of matters in his native land, he brought his accurate knowledge of Greek to bear on the New Testament, and gave forth to Scotland the new information that in Scripture "bishop" and "presbyter" were the same office, and that every minister was a bishop. Modern criticism, even within the fold of the great Anglican Church, to-day says the same thing. But Melville went a good deal further, making this little critical discovery a foothold from which to strike at the whole ecclesiastical fabric. In 1580 he got the General Assembly to accept his views, and to declare further, that the office of "bishop is *unlawful*, and without warrant in the word of God," and he went great lengths in denouncing Episcopal orders.

He was a man of great intellect, ability, learning, and force of character, and he carried the Church with him, which was then in a state of dubiety in which direction to turn. In 1578 he prepared "The Second Book of Discipline," which the General Assembly accepted as supplementary to "The First Book of Discipline," which Knox had compiled. The great feature of Melville's book is that it declares Presbyterianism to be the only divine form of church government, and that it is of "divine right:" the Presbyterian order is the only one commanded in Scripture, and all others are sinful.

It established four great assemblies in the Church, viz., (1) The *General* Council of the whole Catholic Church of God; (2) The *National* or General Assembly of the country; (3) The Provincial Synod; and (4) The Congregational Court, which developed into two lesser assemblies, viz., the Presbytery and Kirk Session.

Not content with the ancient trinity of orders in the Holy Ministry, Melville drew up, from the New Testament, seven orders, not unlike those of the Catholic Apostolic Church of to-day, viz., three *extraordinary* orders, which were only sent forth by God on special occasions and for particular purposes—Apostles, Evangelists, Prophets: and four ordinary orders—the pastor, minister, or bishop—the doctor or divine—the presbyter or elder—and the deacon, to whom pertains the distribution of the Church's alms and the "serving of tables" generally.

Melville was most exclusive and autocratic in his ecclesiastical principles; he was far more particular and precise in regard to the validity of orders and ordination than even Knox had been. He insisted that after a person had been selected for the Holy Ministry, with the consent of the Church, he should then proceed to "*Ordination*," and "the *sanctifying of the person* appointed after trial." The ceremonies at ordination were, fasting, solemn prayer, and the reverent imposition of the hands of the Presbyters. The first reformers had not *insisted* on "the laying on of hands," but it was always practised, though described as "not necessary:" Melville went a step further, and declared it to be "necessary!" and from then till to-day the rite has been strictly observed.

At the Assembly of Dundee in July 1580, the Church proceeded to act on the lines which Melville had learned at Geneva, and *formally abolished the bishops* as a separate order of ministers: "the whole Assembly findeth the same pretended office *unlawful in itself:* and we tell the bishops to quit the same office, and desist from preaching and ministering until they receive, *de novo,* authority from the Church."

In 1581, Melville's "Book of Discipline" was received and sanctioned by the Church of Scotland, as the exponent of its ecclesiastical position and beliefs. In the same year, King James VI., that man of magnificent indiscretion, who now stepped into the monarch's chair, showed his attachment to the Reformed Church by signing "The National Covenant"—or "King's Covenant"—which was a strongly-worded abjuration of Roman doctrines and practices, and an avowal of sympathy with the Reformed order and ritual. He was then only fifteen years old, and was still under Regents. But he had contracted two friendships—one with a young Frenchman, D'Aubigny, and the other with Captain James Stewart, a son of Lord Ochiltree, who ruled his young life and influenced him in favour of the old Roman Faith. The Pope used these two youthful courtiers to work upon the juvenile king; and so, to save him from these evil influences, some of the Protestant lords committed the famous "Raid of Ruthven" (1582), and put James into confinement in Huntingtower, near Perth. It was a very foolish policy. The young king escaped, and then there were apologies all round. But James was impulsive and impetuous, and never forgot the harsh act, nor the impertinence of the Master of Glammis, who, at the royal prisoner's tears, put his foot firmly down, and said, "Better bairns weep than bearded men!" From that day forward, James became the enemy of the Presbyterians.

In 1584 he got Parliament to pass what are called "The Black Acts," by which the king was declared supreme in all things, civil and ecclesiastical; and bishops were re-appointed to exercise the king's spiritual mandates and wishes.

Melville was summoned before the Privy Council, and

ordered to go to Blackness Castle, but he escaped and found refuge at Berwick. The other clergy obeyed the royal command, and a strange order of things supervened— an extraordinary struggle between the two rival systems of Episcopacy and Presbytery.

But James, like Gallio, "cared for none of these things," so long as he had arbitrary power, and plenty of money in his exchequer. To acquire the latter, he got, in 1587, the "*Act of Annexation*" passed, by which the Scottish Crown swept into its coffers all the Church lands and benefices as yet unappropriated; and thus the magnificent properties of the ancient Scottish Church passed into the hands of a king who divided them amongst his rakish favourites, keeping the largest share to himself, "The British Solomon," as he loved to be called—"God's silly vassal," as Melville described him.

It was an age of changes; and in 1590 another came. James, who had married into the royal family of Denmark, turned round again and favoured Presbyterianism. He repealed the "Black Acts," restored Presbyteries, and gave them power to appoint ministers; in a word, Presbyterianism was restored. The year 1592 is famous in the annals of Scotland as the year of the formal establishment of the Presbyterian government of the Church. Another change! Having got the power into their hands, the party of Melville—the Presbyterian High Churchmen who held that only Presbyterians were true Christians—began to *persecute*. They wished the King to send the Northern nobles, who still clung to the Roman Church, into exile, and generally to crush out all other forms of Christianity save their own.

James was disgusted, and the royal weathercock, at this east wind, turned round once more; but this was the last turn! He came to the conclusion that only through bishops could he have his true position as head both of the nation and of the Church. "Presbytery," he said, "agrees as well with Monarchy as God with the Devil;" and so for the last time he embraced the Episcopal form of government, and restored it to Scotland.

At a General Assembly held at Perth, and at another at Dundee, he laid before the Church his proposed plan of restoring the bishops—"not Papistical or Anglican bishops," he said, "but simply spiritual heads and superintendents." Through the influence of the Northern clergy the scheme was carried. In 1603 James succeeded to the throne of England, and two crowns were united on one head; and from that coronation-day he set himself to the great work of assimilating the two countries in religion, faith, law, and ritual!

The outstanding ecclesiastical figure of all this troubled age is Andrew Melville, as John Knox was of the preceding. He was an Ultramontane in every sense of the word—holding that the Church is above all law, and that her province is to give laws, not to obey them. He was a firm, uncompromising, determined man; a born leader of men, prepared for any emergency, fixed in purpose, and composed in spirit, full of divine persistency, and keeping before his eyes only one purpose and object—the dignity, the power, the glorification of the Church. His motto was that of Von Moltke—"First weigh, then venture;" and thus vows ripened into deeds, and decision blossomed into performance! He took the ecclesiastical giant by the throat and threw him, because he had strong convictions and firm resolves, because he had

> "The undivided will;
> 'Tis that *compels* the elements, and wrings
> A human music from the indifferent air!"

Melville was ready either for Holyrood or Blackness—the gown or the gyves—the pulpit or the gallows—if only his own aim and ambition were attained.

It is a wonderful tribute to the power of persistency and consistency; for as Hildebrand made the Church of Rome what it is at this hour so Melville made the Church of Scotland what she practically is at this moment, as she meets in General Assembly in the ancient capital of the Northern Kingdom!

CHAPTER VII.

DARK DAYS.

Episcopacy versus *Presbytery:* 1603—1660.

THE Church of God has from the very beginning been often compared to a ship, of which Christ is the Captain, and which carries men through the troublesome waves of this present world into the peaceful port of Paradise. The very names given by early Christendom to the parts of a church, speak the same thought: the "nave" is simply the "navis" or Latin ship; the "aisles" are the "wings" (alae) or sails of the vessel. As the Christian Father puts it, too, the Church of Christ, like a ship, is small in its beginning, larger in the middle, and then small again at the end, for in the latter days, many shall depart from the faith. Like ships, too, there are different "builds" and orders of churches,—different forms of government, ritual, doctrine; and yet all pointing their prows to the same blessed haven of Eternal Rest! Like the fishing-wherries which you see at evening, when sea and land are flushed with the sunset, all scattered over the Firth, and dotted over the ocean, each intent on its own work, caring little for its neighbour, every hour indeed, as it passes, widening the distance between them; but when they have toiled all night, and the darksome night is passed, morning brings them all together again, and you see them rocking side by side, in crowds, within the stone breakwater; so when the night of life with its struggles and disagreements and efforts is over, the true "Ships of Christ" will find themselves side by side, perhaps to their own great astonishment, and like the

Apostles on Galilee, when the resurrection morning dawns, they will see Jesus Himself standing on the shore!

> "To veer how vain! On, onward strain,
> Brave barks, in light and darkness too:
> Through winds and tides, one compass guides,
> To that and your own selves be true!
>
> But O blithe breeze, and O great seas,
> Though ne'er, that earliest parting past,
> On your wide plain they join again,
> Together lead them home at last!
>
> One port, methought, alike they sought:
> One purpose hold where'er they fare:
> O bounding breeze, O rushing seas,
> At last, at last unite them there!"

The originator of the great "Cunard Line" was a poor Glasgow boy named Sam Cunard, who used to while away his odd hours by whittling out models of little ships with his jack-knife. At last his opportunity came, as it always will come to those who will wait. The great ship-owners, Burns and M'Ivor, desired to increase the speed of their Transatlantic liners, and especially of the mail steamers. Young Samuel Cunard was, by a mere chance, consulted, and he prepared a model of the first "Cunard" steamship. Every one of the magnificent floating palaces of that line is a copy of the carved image which that penniless Glasgow youth prepared in the obscurity of a common lodging-house.

In one respect, every one of our present Scottish parish churches is a copy of the model which Melville prepared in the seclusion of a Genevan college: and not in Scotland only, but scattered all over the civilized world, you see copies of his original. And so with other types of Church order and discipline; in some parts of the world the Ship of Christ is differently constructed, differently rigged, differently navigated from what it is in others. In Scotland, Melville's model has been accepted and reproduced a thousand-fold!

In view of the Dark Days in the story of the Scottish Church, of which we have now to tell, it is a comforting, strengthening, and sustaining thought, that no matter how dark the night, or how rough the sea, or how drenching the rain-storm, the Church's great Head and Master is always near her: His Face shines through the gloom to comfort the storm-tost mariners, and His uplifted Hands can still bless the angry, troubled waters into peace, for His touch has still its ancient power. He can turn the storm into a calm, and say, " Peace, be still!" He can turn the waters of strife into the wine of love: the same power that turned the sweet water of Cana's wells into wine, changed the stormy water of Galilee's lake into calm: whether the water glitter in a jar or roll in an ocean, God is God, and the creature is the creature! The prayer of the Church, therefore, ought to be the prayer of the Breton fishers as they launch out into God's great deep: "My God, protect me: my ship is so little, and Your Sea is so great!"

"The Most High and Mighty Prince, James," had no sooner, "by the grace of God," risen from being ruler of little Scotland and become " King of Great Britain, France, and Ireland,"—"a most Dread Sovereign,"—"the Wonder of the world in this latter age,"—as the translators of his Bible addressed him,—than he resolutely set himself to the work of assimilating the two National Churches of England and Scotland. His recollections of Northern Presbyterianism were *warm*, but not genial: the hearty strokes of George Buchanan's fatherly hand were still tingling in the royal person: the harshness of the " Raid of Ruthven " nobles had passed like iron into the soul: Melville was the Accuser and Nemesis of his life. James always had the will to return an eye for an eye: and now he got the power.

In 1610 a General Assembly was held at Glasgow, where, once more, the bishops were restored, and Presbyterian order thrown out. The Scottish Parliament in 1606 repealed the " Act of Annexation," and the old bishops' lands were thus set free again to be applied to bishops' stipends. But now that bishops were to be restored, who was to consecrate them? Only bishops can make bishops, and Scotland had not a single "father-in-God" to boast of. Three Scottish ministers, therefore,—Spottiswood, Lamb, and Hamilton,—were sent to England and consecrated by the Bishops of London, Ely, and Bath, and they in turn were to consecrate other bishops and to ordain clergy.

To conciliate Melville and win him over to his side, King James asked him up to London, and not only argued with him himself in favour of bishops, but got the most learned divines of the English Church to discuss the question with him. But Melville stuck to his guns and would not give in. In an unfortunate moment, he wrote a squib on the manners of James' Court and the Chapel Royal. James was irritated, and cast the great Scotsman into the Tower, where he remained three long years a prisoner, during which time James and his friends did what they pleased: it was merry with the lambs when the wolf was shut up! He was at last released, and allowed to cross to France to be a professor in the college of Sedan. He never saw Scotland again.

Rid of him, James went further. In 1617 he revisited Scotland, and took up his residence at Holyrood. The old palace-chapel was elaborately fitted up for the great occasion, and an ornate service was carried through. Gathering the new bishops round him, the King explained to them what their duties were to be, and how the worship and discipline of the Church of Scotland were to be conformed to the English use, and closed by ordering them at next General Assembly to carry out these reforms.

A few months later—in 1618—the Assembly met at Perth, and these changes were sanctioned. The chief of them were embodied in the famous "Five Articles of Perth," which were—"1. That the Holy Communion should be received kneeling. 2. That it might be administered in private houses. 3. That Baptism might also be celebrated in private. 4. That all young persons after having learned the Creed, the Lord's Prayer, and Ten Commandments, be brought to a bishop to be confirmed. 5. That the days commemorative of the birth, death, resurrection, and ascension of Christ, and of the descent of the Holy Spirit, be observed as holydays."

It was not that there was so much that was objectionable in these articles,—for most of them are now recognised and practised by the Church of Scotland,—but it was the way in which the whole thing was done. Yet, notwithstanding, the Assembly passed them, and the new regulations came into force. Great confusion was, however, the result in the parish churches of Scotland : and though the whole question was still mainly a clerical one, there was an undercurrent of dissatisfaction among the people.

The crisis came when James I. died, and Charles I. succeeded to the throne. In 1633 he came to Scotland to be crowned with the ancient Scottish diadem, and with him came Bishop Laud, afterwards Primate of all England. On the 23rd of June he attended divine service in St Giles' Church, which he now erected into a cathedral for the Diocese of Edinburgh, and the whole service was conducted according to the English prayer book. While in Edinburgh, the king arranged what for the future were to be the vestments of the clergy in time of worship, and further, to the great disgust of the nobles, tried to get back from them the old Church lands and revenues, and to apply them to their original use—as Episcopal stipends. But the nobles would not give up a farthing, and the result was a severe friction between king and nobility, which came afterwards to a hot, burning head ! And last, but not least, Laud and the Scottish bishops were instructed to prepare a Scottish Liturgy after the Anglican model, only more Roman in tone, which was to supplant the old Reformation Liturgy and Ritual of John Knox, which people and ministers used and loved.

And then the storm broke. On Sunday, July 23rd, 1637, in the Cathedral of St Giles', Dean Hannay, vested in white surplice, began to read the prayer for the seventh Sunday after Trinity :—" Lord of all power and might," &c. The people, whose wrath had been bottled up all the time of these changes, and who very naturally were unwilling to have their fine old National Liturgy supplanted by that of any foreign and exotic Church (for the spirit of Scottish Independence, then as now, was very strong, and the Church of Scotland is just as unwilling to-day to imitate England as it ever was, and wishes all her life, and work, and ritual to be thoroughly national), rose amid a scene of wild uproar. This riot is chronicled in St Giles by a brass tablet inserted near the spot where it occurred. The inscription is, it is understood, from the pen of a distinguished Scotsman, the present Lord Justice-General and Chancellor of the University of Edinburgh: it is as follows:—"Constant oral tradition affirms that near this spot a brave Scotchwoman, Janet Geddes, on the 23rd July, 1637, struck the first blow in the great struggle for freedom of conscience, which after a conflict of half a century ended in the establishment of civil and religious liberty." The "first blow" referred to is said to have been the throwing of the stool on which she was sitting at the head of the officiating clergyman. Whether this be historically correct or not, at anyrate there was something of a riot inside the Cathedral, and a very great riot outside. The new bishops on coming out after this memorable service were hissed and hooted by the mob; and as with one impulse the vast multitude surged around the grey old Cathedral pile, a great civil war was kindled under the shadow of the time-worn fretted crown, which spread all over Scotland, and finally swept across the length and breadth of the whole island. The old St Giles' crown resting on the head of the capital of the country, the ribs of which coronal on festival eves used to be illuminated with coloured lamps and fires, now glowed with the lurid light of revolution—red ruin and the breaking up of laws!

The whole nation then formed itself into what were called "The Tables," which were four associations of different ranks of the community—the clergy, nobles, gentry, and burghers. A bond of union was prepared, called "The National Covenant," in which everyone who signed, promised, while supporting the King and his lawful laws, to preserve their National Independence, and especially the freedom and liberties of the Church. In the old Churchyard of Greyfriars, on the 1st of March, 1638, after a solemn fast, this Solemn League and Covenant was signed, and in a few months the whole country was ready for any emergency.

All that the people asked of the King was that a free General Assembly should be held, and a Special Parliament convened to discuss the affairs of the nation. The request was reluctantly granted by the King's Commissioner, the Marquis of Hamilton. In the venerable Cathedral of Glasgow, that eventful Assembly met on a dark November day in 1638. Alexander Henderson, minister of Leuchars, was chosen Moderator, and Hamilton sat as Royal Commissioner. This Assembly renounced all that had been done during the previous thirty years—the Perth articles, Laud's service-book and canons; and the bishops were deposed and banned. Presbyterianism was once more restored to Scotland and Episcopacy ousted.

Clergy and people were sick of bishops, because of the way in which they had been forced by hook and *crook* upon them, and because they felt that their National Independence was being crippled; and the nobles hated them because they saw that if bishops were to be, bishops must live; and if bishops were to live, *they* would need to refund the Episcopal revenues. No wonder, then, that in the Glasgow Assembly about sixty nobles and gentry sat alongside of the hundred and forty-seven ministers, and banned the bishops—because they loved their revenues.

The result of this most intrepid act of the Scottish General Assembly was a threatened Civil War. The Scottish army, with banners inscribed, "For Christ's Crown and Covenant," encamped at Dunse Law Hill; on the other side lay an English army sent by Charles to punish them. But an agreement was come to, and Charles promised the Scotch all they wanted in the way of a General Assembly and

Parliament. In 1639 this promised Assembly met, and repeated the acts of the Glasgow Assembly, and the Scottish Parliament followed on the same lines. After another threatened armed struggle between King and Covenanters, Charles gave way, and the Covenant triumphed! And he decreed that all members of the Scottish Parliament should sign it, and he himself even went the length of joining in Presbyterian worship.

But there was a heavier storm brewing for King Charles than any that swept over the hills and moors of Caledonia. In 1642 the Great Rebellion broke out in England, and the Puritans under Oliver Cromwell became the dominant party in Church and State. Step by step the king's party was overwhelmed by the Roundheads, until in 1649 they brought Charles to a cruel scaffold, and the Commonwealth was proclaimed!

Scotland and her Church bowed to the English Puritans, and sacrificed all her old traditions, customs, and rites at the bidding of the Westminster Assembly of divines, who drew up the "Confession of Faith," the two Catechisms and the Directory for public worship. The Church of Scotland was *inoculated* for the time with Puritanism, and scant justice and consideration did she get from Oliver Cromwell. Not only were the ancient liturgy and worship and polity of the Scottish Church sacrificed, but even the old broad spirit, which characterised the Church from the first, vanished, and the narrow contracted spirit of English Puritanism, whose god was simply an infinite Oliver Cromwell, which frowned on all life's sinless frivolities, and abhorred the lighter and brighter sides of human life, became characteristic of the Scottish Church.

There was much that was good in it—dogged earnestness, relentless, fearless principle. Even Robert Burns, who was no saint, though a very sweet singer, could say—

> "The solemn league and covenant
> Cost Scotland blood, cost Scotland tears:
> But it sealed freedom's sacred cause:
> If thou'rt a slave indulge thy sneers!"

It was a noble stand for liberty against tyranny, for unflinching principle against lawless passion. Desperate diseases need desperate remedies, and, perhaps, the sour-faced Roundhead was the only man who could do the stern work of a lawless age. But his Christianity was as intolerant as that of Thomas Aquinas, and not half as beautiful: he went through life as if he had killed somebody, and was just returning from the burying of the body: he exactly reversed the fine motto of the great Christian worker—

"Look up and not down :
Look out and not in :
Look forward and not back !"

But the influence added strength and decision and indomitable force to the Scottish character, and more and more the Scottish Church under its spell became like the Scottish Thistle, in its rough independence and impatience of all authority and any interference: "Nemo me impune lacessit !"

CHAPTER VIII.

"NEC TAMEN CONSUMEBATUR."

The Covenanting Struggle: 1660—1688.

"Let Earth and stone still witnes beare
There lies a virgine martyr here,
Murthered for owning Christ supreame
Head of His Church; and no more crime
But not abjuring Presbytery
And her not owning Prelacy,
They her condemned by unjust law.
Of heaven nor hell they stood no awe.
Within the sea, tyed to a stake
She suffered for Christ Jesus sake!
The actors of this cruel crime
Was Lagg, Strachan, Winram and Grahame.
Neither young yeares nor yet old age
Could stop the fury of theer rage.
Here lies Margaret Willson,
Daughter to Gilbert Willson
In Glenvernoch, who was drowned
Anno 1685, aged 18."

A SADDER story than that of the "Wigtoun Martyrs," whose monumental epitaph this is, does not appear on the page of history since that early Christian age, when St Christine, the Roman Patrician's daughter, was for Christ's sake thrown into the Tiber, but who, according to the legend, did not sink, for over her saintly face hovered a misty, gleaming circle of light celestial. Both martyrs have been celebrated by art: the Roman, in the now famous painting of "The Early Christian Martyr" which is to be seen copied and engraved everywhere,—the Scottish in the lovely white marble group that gleams in the peaceful cemetery beneath Stirling Castle.

Between the Roman Christine and the Scottish Margaret there is a chasm of 1300 years: but what is time to Eternal Truth? These two youthful virgin-martyrs join hands across the centuries. As you read the tale of their brief lives, both ending with the Cross, there are still many eyes which are blurred with sudden mists, and the old dusts are roused and stirred by the warm tear-drops; hearts overleap place and age and everything, and you feel that the crowding years are powerless to divide them from your sympathies,—and thus the whole wide world is knit in common brotherhood!

On the 11th of May 1685, a young girl, Margaret Willson, and an old woman, Margaret Lauchlinson, were tied to stakes on the treacherous yellow Solway sands,—and the tide rose upon them,—and, with their latest breath, singing those grand old psalms which speak in so impassioned a strain of that Jerusalem which is above, and *which is free*, and which is the mother of us all, the waters covered them, and they were drowned!

A sharp-witted Scottish sheriff, belonging to the Christian community which was allied with those responsible for this terrible crime, and for the martyrdom, besides, of altogether more than a thousand people, many of them weak women and little children, the banishment of 1700, the imprisonment of other 2800, the extreme persecution of altogether about 18,000 persons, wrote a pamphlet attempting to disprove the historical accuracy of this martyrdom: but no amount of legal acumen and literary smartness could remove the bloodmarks from the door!

If Sheriff Napier's argument is true, then Father Hardouin is also right when on similar sceptical principles he proves that all the Greek and Roman classics were the spurious productious of the thirteenth Christian century; and even Mr Donelly's Cryptogram will have a chance to be accepted as evidence that Bacon and not Shakspere wrote Shakspere!

In the old Greyfriars' Churchyard in Edinburgh, stands the weather-beaten time-worn "Martyrs' Monument,"—marking the spot where many of the Covenanters suffered death. On it we read these words: "From May 27, 1661, that the noble Marquess of Argyle suffered,—to February 17, 1688, that Mr James Renwick suffered, were executed at Edinburgh, about 100 of noblemen, gentlemen, ministers, and others,—noble martyrs of Jesus Christ. The most part of them lie here!"

Scattered across the length and breadth of Scotland, you see many a gray lichen-covered block of stone,—on misty moor and rocky mountain-side,—and in scores of quaint quiet churchyards,—sacred to the memory of one or more of those who were victims during that awful quarter of a century which has been burned into the Scottish memory and branded for ever as "The Killing Time!"

The writer well remembers being taken as a boy to the old house in the moors at Lochgoin, near Eaglesham, on a day of dense gloom and thick hoary mist, and being reverently shown two or three tattered blue flags, on which the words were inscribed, "For Christ's Crown and Covenant," a well-worn Bible, and two or three rusty swords, all Covenanting relics. That the interest in these has not yet died out, was proved by the crowd which was always surrounding the relics of that martyr age, which were on view at the late great Glasgow Exhibition. Call it relic-worship if you please,—and it has already been called so: it is only human! Just as there may be in your house a drawer, the opening of which is to you like the opening again of a little grave, for inside it, thickly covered with the dust of a score of years, lies a broken toy and a withered crust,—links with a childish life, dead long ago: so mankind at large is jealously tenacious of those material links with the past—a flag, a sword, a Bible, a token, a communion cup, a piece of tattered worm-eaten sacramental linen,—these are mute memorials of, and yet living links with, the times that are away and gone!

The Bass Rock is the Patmos of Scotland; many a banished St John has looked out from thence on a sea of blood mingled with fire! Where the screaming sea-fowl wheel in weary circles round that lonely barren rock, and mingle their shrill notes with the deep bass of the German Ocean and the weird moan of the bleak east wind as it rides across the sea, wrapped in *haar*,—there, in the old Castle, whose ruins still cling on to the precipitous slope of the white cliff, hundreds of Scotland's best and bravest were dungeoned! In Dunnottar Castle, a little way from Stonehaven, overhanging the sea, there is still pointed out the "Whigs' Vault," into which a crowd of these poor persecuted creatures were huddled; and it is deeply touching to read of the way in which, by turns, they laid themselves down on the green dripping floor, to catch a breath of the cool sea-breeze as it whistled in through a cranny in the rock!

The writer would very gladly pass over this chapter in the "Story of the Burning Bush," for many reasons: the age was a dark and intolerant one on both sides: to arrive at truth regarding the different movements and doings of that time, requires us to take a great deal off the statements made either by Presbyterian or Episcopal divines. Ardent Presbyterians like Wodrow and M'Crie exaggerate the number of the victims of this age of persecutions, and the terrible details of rapine and ravage over which they gloat, are often founded on the most slender grounds; strongly imaginative pictures being often drawn from shadowy traditions and exceedingly questionable facts. Strong Episcopalians, on the other hand, minimise everything: Sir Walter Scott made fun of the whole affair in his amusing picture of Cuddy Headrigg's mother: some like Sheriff Mark Napier would deny the historic truth of any of these martyrdoms: and where they admit that they did take place, aver that the victims were not religious martyrs and confessors, but simply political offenders who defied king and government, everything and everybody, and who were simply brought to justice, like any other insurrectionists.

The truth lies somewhere between these two extremes: to a very large extent the Covenanters' struggle was political: the west and south of Scotland Whigs were the strong political radicals of their age, who rebelled against imperial despotism and arbitrary government. Underneath the Covenanter's gown there was the political and social reformer, who gave his political views this religious veil: the voice was that of Religion, but the hands were those of Politics.

But he is a shallow reader of history who imagines that having said this, the discussion is closed and the matter is to be hushed up. The very *severity* of the struggle is a proof that religion was at the bottom of it. Religion has been the cause of all the fiercest combats of history. Why? Because men fight most keenly over that which is dearest to them: he loves not God at all, who loves Him not above all, and is willing to shed the last drop of his blood upon the altars of Heaven. A little point of Hindu ritual was the occasion of the Indian Mutiny: the precedence of a Greek or a Roman priest in the Church of the Holy Sepulchre in Jerusalem, of the Crimean War: the precedence of Christ or Cæsar in the Church of Scotland, of the memorable Covenanting struggle.

Controversy is unpleasant and unprofitable, but it is impossible to touch upon this age without raising it; for there is still existing in Scotland a small body of Christians, who, we cheerfully allow, are to-day doing, according to their lights and resources, good Christian work, in a very different spirit, however, from that in which their seventeenth century representatives laboured; but who, we dare not forget, are the ecclesiastical successors of the men who connived at these bloody crimes! Thank God, the Scottish Episcopal Church, though it does not even yet, after the severe lessons of two centuries, seem to have learned that there are higher spiritual gifts than those of narrowness, exclusiveness, and sectarianism—and though, most marvellous to say, it seems to grudge that the National Church of Scotland should have a share in that improvement of ritual, and refinement of religious feeling, life, and work, in which it has itself so largely participated—too largely for the taste of some old-fashioned Episcopalians—improvements and refinements which it was the avowed mission of Episcopacy to introduce and cultivate, and which, having now been accepted, should give joy instead of causing irritation to those who posed as Scotland's æsthetic and catholic teachers; though a "Home-loving Scot," who does not, however, belong to the Church of Scotland but to the "body of Christians calling itself the Scottish Episcopal Church," as it is designated by the law of the land, in paying a visit to the venerable Cathedral of the Northern Metropolis, looks round in horror at a worshipper in St Giles who has in a hurry covered his head before reaching the vestibule, and "is startled into astonishment at the well-known irreverence of his countrymen, but afterwards said with a twinkle in his eye, "Puir creatures! what else could you expect;" though there is still marked room for improvement in the spirit with which that body regards the large Christendom of which it is so small a fragment, thank God it has not yet reached the absurd length of calling itself an *infallible* Church!

The Church like the individual which never changes any of its opinions, never corrects any of its mistakes, and if we mistake not, there are very few indeed, if any, within the pale of that body, who would to-day give the slightest approval to the deeds of which their Episcopal forerunners were the ill-starred and misguided authors! Scottish Episcopacy looking back on its seventeenth century representatives may very well say, "Save me from my friends: surely bloody fathers-in-God have ye been to me!" And the best claim which the Scottish Episcopal Church could advance to-day for that approval and countenance of the Scottish people for which it seems to be so anxious, almost to importunity, sometimes to impertinence: a people who have long since forgiven though they have not forgotten these days, but who still regard that Church as it always did regard it, as an alien and exotic Church, whose bishops —as many writers in the newspaper organ of the body have of late been loudly proclaiming and strenuously lamenting —are foreigners to the land, and ignorant of the history and genius of its people:—a Scottish Episcopalian hardly two months ago declaring in a church paper that "the policy of electing Englishmen to Bishoprics in Scotland, is a policy which appears to me to be *suicidal*, however eminent the individual may be,"—and which, though it claims to be not a dissenting but a "disestablished Church," is so in precisely the same way as the little boy, who, in the schoolmaster's necessary absence, seated himself in the chair of state, and dealt out harsh discipline all round, but who, on the rightful authority's return, was soon driven ignominiously from a position to which he had no earthly claim, and who was well, perhaps too severely, punished for it; the best claim it can advance for Scotland's approval, which it might very well have forfeited for ever, if it has not, is hearty repentance for these terrible deeds of blood in which it was steeped up to the elbows from 1660 till 1688, and an honest statement of its earnest determination to do the work of Christ henceforth in the spirit of Christ's religion of "peace and good will to all mankind," and not in the spirit of narrow Russian Despotism, which gives the knout for everything, or of bigoted Islam, whose great evangelizer is the two-edged blade!

It is with pain that we dip the pen in the ink of controversy: but historical truth is of first importance. It is easy for the Episcopalian to point to the improved ritual of the Scottish Church, and say, "What would Knox say to this?" but much easier for the National churchman to conduct his Episcopal brother back two hundred years, and, pointing to a thousand bleeding martyrs, ask, "What would Christ say to that?" It is more certain, as Hallam puts it, that Christ hates such deeds than that He instituted bishops!

From controversy we gladly pass to historical narrative. In 1660 the Restoration took place; the Puritans were ousted, and Charles II. ascended the throne under magnificent auspices. So joyful was Scotland over the event, that in every church there was a thanksgiving, and even crabbed Jenny Geddes burned her stool and all "her creels, baskets, creepies, and furms," at a royal bonfire which blazed in front of the Tron Church of Edinburgh.

The Church of Scotland was now not only Presbyterian, but strictly Puritan, after the English model. On the Restoration, the ministers appointed the Rev. James Sharp, of Crail, to go to London, and crave the continuance of the Kirk's rights and liberties. Charles' reply was, "We do resolve to protect and preserve the Government of the Church of Scotland, *as it is settled by law*, without violation."

Unfortunately, a few over-zealous Presbyterians drew up a petition praying the king to extirpate Popery, Prelacy, and in fact everything but themselves. When the Scottish Parliament met, it showed a strong reaction from Puritanism. Those who drew up that extreme document were imprisoned: the Marquis of Argyle, who had been the leader in the Covenant, was beheaded, and four days after James Guthrie was executed. In August, Charles restored the bishops, and the crafty Sharp was made Archbishop of St Andrews.

He, together with the saintly Leighton, Fairfoul, and Hamilton, were all consecrated in Westminster Abbey; but Leighton all through not only shrank from the methods of his colleagues, but openly pled for toleration all round. Sharp's aim was to crush Presbytery: and in 1662 an act was passed evicting all ministers who would not submit to the new bishops: three hundred and fifty ministers resigned their livings: the vacancies were filled up with raw curates, in many cases not out of their teens,—mere stipend-lifters who loved the burning Bush for the fruits it bore, not for the Presence that dwelt within it!

Another act was passed compelling the inhabitants of each district to attend church, otherwise the curate would report them for punishment.

Let a hand of mercy draw a veil over that terrible past! To fill the churches, Sir James Turner, Grahame of Claverhouse, the Duke of Lauderdale, and others,—brave soldiers, no doubt, who simply did a soldier's duty (the weight of blame rests not on them so much as on the ecclesiastical system which gave them their instructions), did their work thoroughly. There is not a glen in the South and West of Scotland but has its tradition of death and sorrow!

What deep pathos there is in that "Covenanter's Midnight Hymn" of the Ettrick Shepherd :—

> "O Thou that dwellest in the heavens so high
> Beyond yon star, within yon sky,—
> Where the dazzling fields need no other light,
> Nor the sun by day nor the moon by night;
> Tho' shining millions around Thee stand,
> For the sake of Him at Thy right hand,
> O think of the souls He died for here,
> Thus wandering in darkness, in doubt, and fear!
>
> The powers of darkness are all abroad,
> They own no Saviour, and they fear no God:
> And we are trembling in dumb dismay,
> O turn not Thou Thy Face away!
> Our night is dreary and dim our day,
> And if Thou turnest Thy Face away,
> We are sinful, feeble, and helpless dust,
> And have none to look to and none to trust.
>
> Thy aid, O mighty One, we crave:
> Not shortened is Thy Arm to save:
> Alas! from Thee we now sojourn,
> Return to us, O God, return!"

Charles died on the 6th of February 1685, and James II. succeeded. Matters became even worse, for the king was now a Roman Catholic, and by the "Test Act" even greater severities were practised, and every preacher at conventicles was declared liable to death. And then, once more, man's extremity was God's opportunity: a foreigner stepped in and became the visible hand of the Invisible God. In 1688 William and Mary came to power, and the Revolution Settlement was passed: and it was found that the Burning Bush which had literally blazed with the fierce fires of persecution for a quarter of a century, *was yet not consumed:* "nec tamen consumebatur." It must have been in this age that the Church took that as its crest.

The last martyr, James Renwick, went to the scaffold on February 18th, 1688, with these words on his lips : "Yonder is the welcome warning to my marriage: the Bridegroom is coming: I am ready: I am ready!" This was the last crush of the grapes! The blood of the martyrs is the seed of the Church: they lit a candle in Scotland which will never be put out: from every drop of their blood, as of old, an armed host has sprung up: they won the day, but as Wellington said after a hard-earned victory, " Another such victory, and our army is gone!"

CHAPTER IX.

PEACE WITH HONOUR.

The Revolution Settlement: 1688.

So reckless and despotic did the conduct of James II. become, that at last both England and Scotland rose as one man. The next heir to the throne was William Prince of Orange; but just before the climax, James' queen gave birth to an infant prince, by which the Dutchman's claims to the throne were negatived. But justice is above heredity: and when the seven English bishops, who had been committed to the Tower for refusing to read the despot's indulgence from their pulpits, were acquitted, the nation gave such evident signs of jubilation and of rebellion against absolutism, that William saw that his hour had come. He marked that the English Church and people were against James, and that the Scottish Church and people, with the exception of those who held comfortable and lucrative offices, were in a state of revolution: and so, seeing that the royal infant stood between him and the throne, after earnest solicitation and entreaty he crossed from Holland, and landed at Torbay on November 4, 1688—just two hundred years ago! There was no opposition, save that the Scottish Council made an offer of their lives and fortunes to the ousted king, and refused to circulate William's Royal Proclamation. Only the day before the Scottish bishops wrote a fulsome letter to King James, in which he was eulogized as "the darling of heaven," and God was asked to give him "the hearts of his subjects and the necks of his enemies," allegiance to his royal person being declared to be "an essential part of their religion."

It was a dark day for the Scotch Episcopal body, as the writer has more than once heard from its pulpits, when it identified itself with a monarchy so oppressive, against which at last the entire island rose. From that day forward the Scotch Episcopalians became identified with the Stuarts, and clung to the hope with a most affecting persistency, that some day, somehow, the true seed royal would be restored! After all danger was over, one may cheerfully allow that there was something almost beautiful in their impassioned devotion to the old line: but it was death to their Church, as some of their own bishops have admitted. Their adherence through storm and sunshine to the Stuart dynasty brought on them many a sorrow and much persecution. Refusing to acknowledge and to pray for the king, they were treated as political rebels, and their worship was forbidden: and when through dire necessity they were constrained, for bare life, to acknowledge the king and the princely line which the nation had chosen, it was with a very bad grace, and done generally in the clever and double way of old Dr Byrom's couplet :—

> " God bless the king : God bless the Faith's Defender !
> God bless,—no harm in blessing the 'Pretender' !
> Who that Pretender is, and who that king,—
> God bless us all,—is quite another thing ! "

The romance was deepened in the days of Prince Charlie; and the way in which the Episcopalian Jacobites immortalized him in the sweetest lyrics ever breathed in any land, and treasured for generations the smallest relics of his royal presence and graceful personality (witness the glistening golden lock of hair in the possession of which Sir Walter Scott gloried at Abbotsford), and hoarded up the scraps of his handwriting and bits of his attire, which are even yet disclosed to favourites' by ardent Jacobites; and the clinging love with which any ancestral personal relations to the Lord's Anointed King of Scotland are still cherished and handed down, is proof of the intensity and reality of the feeling. Dr Chalmers paid a visit to old Mrs Elizabeth Drew, who died near Glasgow, in 1821, at the great age of 102, to hear from her own lips the graphic story of how, when she was a girl in 1746, the fair Prince and the "rebels" visited the Drews' farm of Bogleshole near Campsie, and demanded shelter and food: and how, as the rough soldiers held up lumps of cheese on their bayonet-points to roast at the fire, Prince Charlie came up to her as she was sitting at the hearth, and gently stroked her hair. That touch became the one pride and glory of her life. And traditions such as these were warmly cherished by those who clung to the Stuart line. Poetry, however, is one thing,—plain prose another! And if James II. had not been so ill-advised, so wickedly blind, guilty of such magnificent indiscretions, so unlike the right, true king, who dares do aught save wrong,—but who, on the contrary, took the sword against his own people, and therefore perished by the sword, according to divine law; had he been but moderately reasonable in his demands, and decently humane in his measures, the Stuart ensign would still be floating over the dark palace of Holyrood and the gray towers of Windsor.

After a short struggle, James II. fled to France; the island hissed a curse after him, and William and Mary quietly ascended the throne. The great question which now agitated Scotland was—what was to be the relation of the new monarch to religion? William of Orange was brought up in the National Presbyterian Church of Holland, which is still the Church of that country; but beyond this he seems to have cared very little whether the Church was governed by presbyters or bishops, provided the Crown was supreme. All he wanted was to have Scotland loyal to his throne and person, and for his part he would give them either presbyterian or episcopal government according to the nation's will; but—and here was the grand principle of his rule—*there was to be no more persecution for religion!* Mr Ruskin, speaking of a certain tribe of bees, says, "They will steal each other's nests like human beings, and fight like Christians;" and a great Scottish humorist speaks of a dog which he knew, whose life was full of seriousness, because he could not get enough of fighting! The crest of Christianity is not a clenched fist, but two joined hands: and William, who came to Scotland fresh from other scenes, looked with other eyes than theirs, and desired to make allowance for them all. The great glory of the Revolution is not the establishment of one form of church government or another, but the complete discountenance and annihilation of religious persecution. Scotland drew a long breath when William sat down on the old Scottish "crowning stane," and called her ancient Regalia his own!

Granted this principle, however, of toleration and moderation, the rest was to William a matter of entire indifference. "Which of you," he asked, "will support me most loyally?" In London, both Presbyterians and Episcopalians had their deputations ready to meet him. The great Presbyterian Churchman, William Carstares, who is the one grand central ecclesiastical figure of this epoch, and who himself had suffered thumbscrews, imprisonment, and exile, who had been with William in Holland for long advising him as to how and when he should claim the throne of the British Islands, and had crossed with the Prince in the same ship to Torbay, and been the religious guide and pastor of William's army, stated clearly and moderately the claims of the Presbyterians. Bishop Rose, whose Episcopal chair stood in St Giles' Cathedral, Edinburgh, along with Sir George Mackenzie, stated the Episcopalian position. To Bishop Rose, the king put one crucial query: "You will be good to me in Scotland and follow the example of England?" "Sir," was the bishop's brave though disastrous reply, "I will serve you as far as law, reason, or conscience shall allow me," that was to say—not at all! Surely in after days, as he ministered in his obscure little chapel in old Carrubber's Close, after being ejected from the Cathedral, he must often have regretted that memorable speech, when with a very little conciliatoriness and tact, he might, in the political upheaval, have brought his own Church into royal favour and possibly into popular repute. His answer sealed the fate of the Scottish bishops: William summoned a convention of Scottish estates in March 1689; one hundred and fifty members were present, including the seven bishops: all accepted William as their Sovereign save nine, and of these only two were not prelates. William took the oath, but at the last clause which bound him to root out all heretics, "I will not," said he, "lay myself under any obligation to be a persecutor!" And with this understanding he was allowed to swear.

The Convention's next act was to remove the bishops from the Church of Scotland, and to declare that the ancient Church of the country would for the future be without any superintending pastors. They had miserably failed to secure respect and confidence, save one whose memory comes across the ages even yet like a breath of sweet incense,—Scotland's Apostle of Peace, Archbishop Leighton; and he thought so much of his Episcopal associates that he left them, in order that the government of the Church might be carried on, on more democratic lines, by councils and assemblies of the presbyters themselves!

Practically it made little or no difference to the Church as an ecclesiastical body: it was the same *Church* all through — the same apostolic succession in the Holy Ministry, only during the brief episcopal *régimes*, presbyters were ordained by the bishop who was invested for the time with the authority of the entire presbytery: but now, as at previous times, the presbytery took the power of ordination and other powers which it had deputed to the bishop, upon itself to be exercised by itself. The General Assembly had never ceased to exist even when the bishops were in power, and seemed to make it superfluous; and the practical work of the Church and her ritual were the same under both forms of government. Scottish Episcopacy then used no prayer book, and had no outward marks of difference in ritual from the ordinary Presbyterian service: the only difference between the two rivals was the existence or absence of a chief shepherd over the under-shepherds! And what William did was merely to modify the government of Scotland's ancient Church, and not, as an English Church paper lately said in describing the difference between the Established Church of England and the Established Church of Scotland—to affirm that the former Church was the ancient branch of the Catholic Church in the southern end of the island, dating from apostolic times, and that the latter was an institution created by Parliament in 1688!!! No statement could be more untrue and unjust. Truly in a far deeper sense than the South has ever realised, the Church of Scotland has maintained her spiritual independence, having fought against parliament, privy council, crown, everybody, to save what she, with touching simplicity, called "the Crown Rights of her Redeemer!" It is true, her very independence has won the respect and countenance of the Crown to a far greater extent than even the Church of England enjoys, and an outsider might mistake these state recognitions for signs of the Church's slavery and submission. One of the most approved organs of advanced Anglicanism lately declared, with some degree of envy, in view of the present strained relations between extreme ritualists in the South and the Sovereign who is the head of their Communion that "the Scottish Kirk had come out of the struggle with the state with far more material honours even, than the English Establishment." "Witness," it said, "the imposing State ceremonial with which the annual spiritual congress or assembly of the National Church is honoured, and the representative presence of the Sovereign herself. We have lost that, as well as a host of other privileges which the Scottish Kirk has got."

It is high time that that remark were smothered regarding the civil and state origin of the Scottish Church: no church ever showed such a fierce independence and determined dogged opposition to the least touch or tickle of the State's little finger. So fiercely did she turn on any prince or prince's representative who dared to breathe that he, and not Christ, would rule her in the minutest detail of her spiritual work, that at last kings and princes and governments gave up troubling her, in disgust, as past all curing and all controlling, and allowed her to rule herself according to her own sweet will. And all that her critics can say of her to-day is, "We do not understand, and do not wish to understand, Scottish affairs!" The basis of the "Revolution Settlement," which put the Church of Scotland finally on the Presbyterian foundation on which it still rests, is the famous "Claim of Right," by which the Episcopate as an order was deleted from Scottish Church Polity. All the parish clergymen retained their charges, save only where they would not take the oath of allegiance to the Crown. There can be little doubt that, although no direct *persecutions* were indulged in by the Presbyterian party, many of their fellow-churchmen who were suspected of a leaning to Episcopacy, were treated with unnecessary harshness.

It was a nasty age, and neither side was remarkable for that which is above all Churches and Creeds, "the greatest of these," which is charity. We have only to read some of the sermons of the period to see the temper of the time: the Cameronians were raging because William would not keep the "Covenant" and extirpate everybody but themselves. "What did the Puritans go to America for?" was once asked in a school: and the answer was, "To worship God in their own way, and *make other people do the same!*" That was precisely the spirit of the Revolution age; and because the politic Dutchman would not espouse their side, the ultra-presbyterians, like Shields and Rule, spoke familiarly of him as one who "was rather seeking an earthly crown to himself than seeking to put the crown on Christ's head:" and that "King William designed to dethrone King Jesus." "Good Lord," the same divine once prayed at Dumfries, "bless the king with *a stated opposition in his heart to the antichristian Church of England,* and with *grace to destroy* all the idolatry and superstitions of their foolish and foppish worship: that so we may all be united in the bond of the solemn league and covenant, and purified *according to that pattern in the mount!*" "No king," said another, in the Edinburgh Tron Church, "has any power even to adjourn the General Assembly, but King Jesus!" At last these speeches reached the king's ears, and his strong Dutch countenance, which at all times had about it the look of a thunderstorm asleep, fell in anger; a crisis between the Crown and the Church was imminent. The Crown claimed the right of calling the Assembly together, and the Royal High Commissioner on February 13th, 1692, dissolved the Assembly in the king's name, and refused to name the next day of meeting. Nemo me impune lacessit! With calm determination, the moderator, "in the name of the Lord Jesus Christ, *the sole head of His Church,*" fixed the next meeting for August 1693. Parliament intervened, and besides arranging about the summoning of the Assembly by the sovereign, drew up the "oath of assurance," by which Episcopal ministers could take Scotch incumbencies on signing the declaration that William was king both *de facto* and *de jure*, and requiring all members of Assembly to take this oath!

And now came the crisis on which the fortunes of the Church of Scotland hung. The Church resolutely refused to be dictated to by the Crown: the Crown ordered the Commissioner to summon the Assembly for 29th March 1694, and then to make each member take the oath of allegiance, and if the Assembly refused, to dissolve it! Neither Church nor Crown would give way! Principal Carstares at this momentous crisis stepped in as deliverer. Taking advantage of his long standing intimacy with the king, he hurried up to London, arriving late at night. Not a moment was to be lost, for the Assembly would meet in a few days, and if William would not give in a little, there would be a national disaster. When Carstares arrived at Kensington, the king was in bed, sound asleep: but the indomitable Scotsman sent in word that he must see the king. The servants opened the royal chamber door, and the king was lying asleep. Carstares drew the bed-curtain aside and touched him, the king turned round and gazed at him, in astonishment to see him there and so late. "I have come," said the noble principal, "to ask my life!" "And is it possible," William responded, "that you have been guilty of a crime deserving death?" Carstares then told him how he had *taken upon him to stop the king's letter*, containing his peremptory injunction to the Lord High Commissioner as to his procedure. "Have you indeed," said William with a frown, "dared to countermand my orders?" Carstares fell on his knees and told his story, of how the Scottish Church was in peril, and if the king's word as stated in the letter were carried out, the Scottish Church would in a few days be in ruins! And he pled so hard, that the king bade him throw his letter into the fire, and the two of them sat down and drew up a more moderate mandate, in which the king dispensed with the oath, and gave the Church her ancient rights and privileges. William signed it hurriedly, and at dead of night a messenger was dispatched in fearful haste to Scotland. He arrived in Edinburgh, carrying in his hand what was as really a reprieve as the other letter was a warrant for execution, just a few hours before the great bell of St Giles' Cathedral was tolling for the opening service of the Assembly. That letter saved the Church; it was read to the Assembly, which met that morning trembling for the Church's future: and once and for ever, the relations of Crown and Church were fixed and settled, to the satisfaction of both.

It was Carstares' strong wisdom and wonderful bravery and pluck that saved the Scottish Church. He was a man of purpose and of will, and he wrested the Church's rights and liberties out of a granite hand. His life was a piece of visible rhetoric, a sermon in dust and ashes, on the poet's text,

> "Be you like your mountain oak,
> Of sturdy mien, in purpose strong,
> And prove thyself to be unchanged
> In every sense from right to wrong.
> Let not success unbalance mind;
> In adverse times be honest then,
> Support the truth, and thou shalt march,
> A monarch, in the van of men!"

CHAPTER X.

"AND THE LAND HAD REST."

The Church of the Eighteenth Century: 1690—1800.

"BLESSED is the nation which has no history," is a beatitude which sounds also like a paradox. But when one remembers that history speaks mostly of storms and unrest,—battles and marches, toils and moils, changes and chances,—while seasons of serenity and peace are passed over in a sentence, its truth is flashed home on the mind. One of the most tragic and sensational of modern novelists declares that if it were not for these lulls and dead pauses, and deep parentheses of silence—periods of seeming dulness perhaps—our little lives would be hell, because our souls would be kept perpetually bubbling and boiling in the huge pot of existence, heated with thorns and coals of juniper. The calms that come in his thrilling stories, may be unfortunate for the readers, but they are fortunate for the *read;* for excitement is not the normal condition of the human subject, and the historian who only gives you the story of Red Ruin, and the shock of war, and the crack of doom, and, in the individual life, of existence at high pressure, rushing gasping across the arena—burning the oil at an extravagant rate—is not a true historian :

> " For all our life is made of little things :
> Our chain of life is forged of little rings :
> And little words and acts uplift the soul ! "

The times of Blessedness in the history of a man or a nation are the times of stillness : "in quietness and confidence shall be your strength." Storm is not the normal state of the atmosphere; storm and stress in nature have their function, but nature can no more live on storm and stress, than man, the *make* of whose soul is immortal, can live on bread alone. The creative, the beneficent forces of the universe are all quiet, silent, gentle; the sweet influences of spring—as, crowned once more with violets and mist, and flushed with the rose of newly-wakened consciousness, she wanders in at the open door and throws a snowdrop down on the cold lip of the snow-wreath—the lion and the lamb lying down together—are far more lastingly potent than the grand progress of the storm-fiends across ocean and continent, levelling the forests and shattering the fleets, sending the hapless ship tearing across the wild chaos of winds and waves like a scared bird, with its feathers all drenched and ruffled, hurried along it knows not to what doom—and then, having done their awful work on the restless ocean, passing away inland, with an ominous howl and a low wolf-like roar, to have a night of it among the hills!

The silences of history and of life are as eloquent as their utterances! At the burning of Moscow, the sublimity of the scene was so overpowering that the gazing crowds stood mute; after the greatest of German musicians on one occasion ceased to play, there was a dead pause of reverential admiration through the room; when the Long Parliament met to condemn Strafford to the scaffold, prayers being ended, a solemn silence ensued, and no one had the courage to proceed.

> " I yield due praise
> Unto your bellowing orator; and yet
> How grand is silence! In her tranquil deeps
> What mighty things are born!"

One of the greatest advances of modern historical science, is the deeper realization which our best historians have come to, of the fact that the story of a nation's peace is as important, if not more so, than the story of a nation's wars and strife. It is best when there is not much to record, because it is then that most of what is good and great and true is accomplished. The creation of this beautiful universe is dismissed in one short chapter of the Bible; the Great All-Father whispered and worlds awoke out of nothingness; thirty-one verses of the Holy Book are all the record that lives of the grandest, the greatest, in comparison with everything else, the *only* event of Time worth recording; the other 1188 chapters are the narrative of the little doings and sayings of an ephemeral race of creatures on one of the smaller planets in one of the smallest systems of that universe! Chapter after chapter of the books of "Joshua" and "Judges" teems with stirring narrations of the valorous deeds of a Barak, a Jael, and a Gideon; but the happy peace and sunshine of more than a generation is covered by the single verse—" And the land had rest forty years."

And yet in history, the true life of a nation is nourished, fostered, and developed in these years of halcyon calm; wars are the physic—peace is the health of a people; happiness, like light, is colourless when unbroken. In the monastic annals there is not one single reference to the epoch-making Battle of Poitiers in 732, which effectually checked the spread of Mohammedanism across Europe, and saved the west from being brought under the sway of the Crescent instead of the Cross; but these cloister chronicles teem instead with small petty details, temporal and spiritual, of the life of great calm and peace divine, spent in the dim retreats of many a gothic monastery. And who shall say which events are the more important—the story of war or the story of worship—and which the more useful in the history of a nation or an individual—the life of stir or the life of silence!

> " Star differs from star in glory,
> Moving o'er the self same sky;
> Saint varies from saint in glory,
> As they pass the same Altars by!"

And so different men are born for different ages and different purposes; and different historical movements are sent for particular moral and spiritual ends. All these movements and all the moving spirits in them have their function and their place; but let not the seemingly lean ears despise the full ears,—let not the sword despise the plough, or the helmet the cowl. For, for the Christian spirit, everything is for the best, and everything is beautiful in that web of Providence which is woven by the Hand of Mercy, and by the eternal command and will of Heaven, " while the earth remaineth, seedtime and harvest,"—years of quiet sowing and preparation, and the years of glorious golden fruition and ingathering;—" cold and heat,"—epochs of seeming stagnation but really of quiet usefulness, as well as times when a nation's life-blood runs warm and the fire is in the veins;—" day and night,"—periods of great spiritual and intellectual illumination, as well as periods of religious rest and refreshment;—" summer and winter,"—ages of universal awakening and world-wide life, as well as ages when individual soul-gardening is more practised, and the spirit sits at its own hearthstone, and, Mary-like, learns of God, hearing outside the moaning wail of life's storm as it sighs plaintively through the forest of mortality, in which it knows full well not to build its nest, for it is a forest sold to Death;—" while the Earth remaineth, none of these shall cease!"

The eighteenth century was, for the Church of Scotland, an age of quiet usefulness and latent power. There is very little to record about her, save onward progress and steady consolidation. In 1707, Scotland and England became really one country—united not only in Crown but in Parliament. Scotland ceased to be a separate political power; but careful provision was made for the preservation of all her ancient and time-honoured institutions. Those in our time who desire Scotland to be even more distinct as a nationality than she is at present, should be the first to stretch out a hand to save the Scottish Ark of God from falling, or from being carried away south by English Philistines!

If you except the Church of Scotland, the Court of Session, the Universities, and, above all, the Scottish character with its grit, its determination, its sturdy independence, its deep-seated religious principle and reverence for the Unseen,—so marked that at the late Tercentenary of Edinburgh University, foreign scholars and *savants* were struck at the place of honour which was accorded to religion, even in our secular assemblages; if you except these, and especially the first of them, which has been the making of the others and of them all, and the very palladium of our liberties, there is little else distinctively Scottish left us to-day!

Nothing is more striking than the force and determination of the language used in the "Act of Union," passed in 1707, regarding the perpetual obligation laid upon crown, parliament, and people, to defend and preserve for ever our Ancient Scottish Zion. So deeply important was the subject that the ordinary Commissioners for Union were not allowed to treat of it: it was made a special subject of inquiry by Queen Anne and her Parliament. Never can Scotland throw aside that obligation, as stated in the following trenchant sentences:—"It being reasonable and necessary that the true Protestant Religion as presently professed within this kingdom, with the worship, discipline, and government of this Church, should be effectually and *unalterably* secured: therefore her Majesty, with advice and consent of the said estates of Parliament, doth hereby establish and confirm the said true Protestant religion, and the worship, discipline, and government of this Church *to the people of this land, in all succeeding generations.* And lastly, that after the decease of her present Majesty (whom God long preserve), the sovereign succeeding to her in the Royal Government of this Kingdom of Great Britain, shall in all time coming at his or her accession to the crown, *swear and subscribe that they shall inviolably maintain and preserve the foresaid settlement* of the true Protestant religion, with the government, worship, discipline, rights, and privileges of this Church, as above established by the laws of this kingdom, in prosecution of the Claim of Right. *It shall be held in all time coming as a fundamental and essential condition of any treaty of union to be concluded betwixt the kingdoms, without any alteration thereof, or derogation thereto, in any sort for ever !"*

Nothing could be more painfully distinct than the fact, that, according to law, the hand that would tear down our Scottish churches and cathedrals, must first tear down the crown: for the most august member of the Church of Scotland at this hour wears her crown and holds her sceptre over the Northern Kingdom on this one condition —*the first Coronation Oath in Westminster Abbey*—that she is true (as thank God she so abundantly is) to the Church of our ancestors and the Faith of our fathers!

The second great event of this period was the Revival of Patronage in the Church. Ever since the Reformation it had been a recognised principle, as stated in Knox's "First Book of Discipline,"—"the right of every several congregation to elect their ministers." Patronage had been revived occasionally during Episcopal times, but for more than two generations it had been unknown. On April 22nd, 1712, the "Act of Queen Anne" was passed by both Houses of Parliament, by large majorities, restoring Patronage. Henceforth, heritors were to appoint clergymen, and the congregations were to accept their nominees as a matter of course. Here is the root and beginning of all Scottish Nonconformity. The Church of Scotland resisted the Act bravely: forty presbyteries petitioned and demonstrated against it: for twenty years the Church Courts fought vigorously: and then from 1730 to 1770 secessions began to take place, in consequence of unacceptable ministers being thrust in on the people. This Act has been Scotland's curse, for it has been the cause of the two large secessions, the representatives of which are still to the fore, as well as of a multitude of little sects which have long since died out.

In my next chapter I shall deal with Scottish Nonconformity,—its cause, and how that cause has been so happily removed: and now pass to the general religious movements of this interesting period. It was in this age that the two classes of Christians received their names of "moderate" and "evangelical." The moderate clergy showed sympathy with a larger, broader Christianity than had hitherto prevailed in Scotland: they did not so much mind for *pure* Christianity as for *applied* Christianity. In their preaching they treated of death and life, hell and judgment, providence and virtue, the rewards of the blessed, and the like.

Perhaps they erred too much in neglecting the grand truths and doctrines of the Holy Catholic Church: for example, David Hume once said to Alexander Carlyle, the famous minister of Inveresk (who was rebuked by his presbytery for going to the theatre to see Home's "Douglas"),—after hearing him preach a sermon in the pulpit of that dramatist in Haddingtonshire,—"What do you mean by treating John Home's people to-day to one of Cicero's Academics? I did not think such heathen morality could have passed in East Lothian!"

Read Dr Blair's "Sermons," and you will see the usual type of moderate preaching,—beautiful in style, commonsense in tone, but somewhat lacking in force and fervour! The serious charge has, however, been brought against it that it veiled the Cross and discrowned the Saviour. "O Virtue," cried Blair in his famous sermon in the Old Greyfriars, Edinburgh, "if thou wert embodied, all men would love thee!" In the afternoon of the same day, his colleague, the Rev. R. Walker, a strong evangelical, in the course of his sermon remarked:—"My reverend friend observed in the morning that if virtue were embodied all men would love her. Virtue has been embodied; but how was she treated? Did all men love her? No! she was despised and rejected of men, who, after defaming, insulting, and scourging her, led her to Calvary, where they crucified her between two thieves!"

Too much has, however, been made of the "cold morality" of the moderates who were termed "innocent preachers."

No doubt morality rather than Christian doctrine occupied their attention, and too much they forgot those Catholic truths, of which the Church of God is the "pillar and ground,"—the "pillar" on which is hung the glorious proclamation of God's pardon and Christ's peace, the "ground" or Borestone in which the Banner of the Cross is fixed.

Moral truth, scientific research, human wisdom of every kind are all included in the majestic sweep of Christianity; but there is a *Sun* beyond the sun, and the hum of a music celestial beyond the music of the spheres—

> " Let science without revelation
> About its hypothesis prate :
> It sports at the threshold of knowledge
> But never can open the gate !"

The Evangelicals, on the other hand, frowned on literature and art, and formed the narrow Puritanical element in the Church. Thus there came to be a great cleavage between the two parties,—a cleavage which still exists in remote quarters of the West Highlands,—where even yet the most extreme term of reprobation for any person is to call him a "Mōderate." The separation culminated in 1843 when the "High-Fliers," or extreme evangelicals, seceded from the Church : and it is very amusing even yet to see, in the North and North-West of Scotland,—especially in the island of Lewis,—how the so-called "Evangelicals" keep aloof from the so-called Moderates,—not recognising them on the road even when *driving to a communion*, and avoiding them like sin,—with the plain object, of course, of keeping up the old bitterness and separatist feeling in the minds of their people.

It is not so many years since schoolboys in Ross, coming in late for school, used, when asked if they did not "hear the horn," to plead as an excuse that (if they were Free Church) "they thocht it was the Mōderate Horn," and the Moderate boys pled guilty to the soft impeachment that they thought the horn heard by them had been the " Free Horn," —so tossed were the dear boys on the two horns of the Northern dilemma !

Tourists, railways, and the schoolmaster are gradually clearing out all that nonsense,—and to-day there are very few enlightened Scotsmen who, while regretting the defective Catholic teaching of the Moderate pulpit, do not admire the literary excellences of Robertson, Blair, Campbell, Jupiter Carlyle, Horne, Reid, Webster, Witherspoon, and quite a galaxy of other names distinguished in the Republic of Letters. The Moderate clergy furnished, in the great majority of cases, splendid types of noble, consistent Christian living,—men who preached without ever saying a word; and though ignorant and illiterate extremists may easily find joints in their armour, they cannot strip them of those peerless virtues of peaceableness, toleration, and human kindliness, for which they were so distinguished!

A true Church should have the kernel of evangelical truth in the shell of apostolic order: but during this age, ritual, doctrine, and practical work were sorely neglected. The Divine Offices of the sanctuary were bald and barren: the House of God was a house of gloom, and the ancient glories of Scotland's worship were hopes that died to rise in memories!

The Holy Scriptures, man's guide-book to Heaven, ceased to be read in churches. The most glorious portrait in that Album of heaven,—the portrait of the Thorn-crowned—"the fairest among sons of men and the Altogether Lovely,"—was hurriedly passed over, or at best that sorrowful face which gleams across the centuries was only one of a galaxy of kindred Masters of Religion. And the solemn Eucharistic Memorial of a Saviour's dying love was neglected, and when celebrated, celebrated with no reverence, and the scantiest decency. In 1796 a debate took place in the General Assembly, as to whether missions to the heathen were right or wrong,—a very elementary question for those who had Christ's "marching-orders" in their hand,—and the friends of missions were defeated!

The relation of the Church to the rest of Catholic Christendom was forgotten, and a strong provincialism was engendered. And yet the Church of England was in exactly the same position: indeed, according to the Philosophy of History, it was just that "*the land had rest*" after a long period of war and tumult,—and on the eve of new trials: for in the Church as in the individual, a rest is given only to prepare and stimulate it for further exertion and endurance.

And so the eighteenth century glided by (not without a stirring movement which will find its due place in next chapter), but for the most part silent-footed and swift-winged: for when "the land has rest," and (to use the quaint expression of the old Paraphrase) they "hang the trumpet in the hall,"—then

> "Years roll through the palm of ages
> As the dropping rosary speeds,
> Through the cold and passive fingers
> Of a hermit at his beads!"

CHAPTER XI.

"THAT THEY ALL MAY BE ONE."

Scottish Nonconformity and its Cause.

THE year of grace, 1888, bids fair to be famous in the history of Christendom as the year of general councils and synods. In the great Eastern Church, a memorable synod has been held in Russia, in celebration of the seventh centenary of the Christianizing of that vast empire. At that great assembly, attended by patriarchs and prelates from every part of the Czar's dominions, there have been evidences of a renewed spiritual life which has long been wanting, and unmistakeable proofs, that though still the Greek creed denies the Procession of the Holy Spirit from the Son, but declares it to be "of the Father only," thus breaking away from Catholic truth, and laying a doctrinal foundation for that spiritual torpor which has so long reigned in the Oriental communion—nevertheless, the spirit of the Lord Jesus Christ, which is a spirit of unity, peace, and concord, is increasingly present in that region of Christ's universal empire, filling the hearts of the pastors of Christ's flock in Russia, Siberia, and the East!

The second great ecclesiastical council of 1888 has been the Lambeth Conference, attended by one hundred and fifty bishops from every part of the world—chief pastors even from the negro states of America attending, and sitting down in solemn conclave alongside of the Protestant Bishop of Jerusalem, and that dark Syrian prelate who attracted so much notice from his supposed strong resemblance to Him who eighteen hundred years ago breathed thirty blessed years under the Syrian blue. The tone of the assembly was lofty and Christ-like; and not the least important of their deliberations concerned the reunion of Christendom—the judgment of the Council being that every possible concession should be made to other branches of Christ's Church, with a view to the accomplishment of Christ's dying wish and prayer—"that they all may be one": and, in order to carry out these recommendations, a committee was formed, presided over by one whose praise is in all the churches, the venerable and venerated Bishop Wordsworth of St Andrews. "The power of Christ" was the grand subject of the Archbishop of York's closing sermon to that hundred and fifty chief shepherds from every land and clime, in St Paul's Cathedral. Surely the prayers of that unique assembly, which the head of the Old Catholic movement has declared that he envies, and which, had it come sooner, might have spared Christendom another sect—the Old Catholics—will not be unheeded and unanswered by the Church's Head which suffers untold sorrow when it feels the *knife* at work among the members!

The third assembly of 1888 has been the Pan-Presbyterian Council, held in London, and including representatives from all Christian lands, when the affairs of those vast Christian communities whose church government is according to *presbyters*, were discussed. The same broad spirit characterized its proceedings, and there seemed to be a general thirst for unity. "Amongst Presbyterians," said Principal Oswald Dykes, "the forces of *Disruption* have now spent themselves, and we are beginning a new era of peace and life!"

It would thus seem that East and West are at last conspiring together for the reunion of Christendom: we seem to be on the eve of a great and universal *foregathering* of the whole flock of Jesus. The days have now almost slipped by, when it is possible to hear any more the old Scotch elder's prayer,—"O Lord, grant that we may be right, for Thou knowest we are very decided," or that other worthy's petition that Heaven would bless himself and family,—"us four and no more! We are beginning, though slowly, to find out that what we took for a monster, through the fog of controversy, was really our own Christian brother, and that, as has more than once happened in practical warfare, we have through the mists been pounding away vigorously at detachments of our own forces.

There are very few good people now who wish to glean up the shafts which lie scattered all over the battlefields of religion, and to use them over again: "there let them lay," is the one absorbing wish and prayer! We have all made the naked scimitar too much the object of our religious worship, and to-day a deep, agonizing impassioned wish seems to be thrilling through the globe, for the removal of that horrible emblem from God's Altar, and the substitution of the holy symbol of Christ's Cross, which holds out its peaceful arms as if to embrace the whole world, which points in every direction of space, as if to show that it is for all climes, and which, though planted in the earth, points to the eternal skies, where, beyond these voices, there is peace!

Charles Kingsley's last death-bed murmur is the murmur which to-day rises from all the Churches of Christendom, "No more fighting! No more fighting!" Even the Roman Church cannot escape the sentiment which is rising steadily every day, so that even the Vatican is broadening when a cheap translation of the gospels into French, of which 144,000 were sold in France within the year, received the Papal imprimatur and blessing. In the late Pilgrimage to Iona, when the weather-beaten tower of St Columba's old cathedral rose above the edge of the sea-line, the rocky shores of Mull were made to echo with the stirring strains of Faber's famous hymn, which the pilgrims sang:—

> " Faith of our Fathers! we will love
> Both friend and foe in all our strife
> And preach thee too, as love knows how
> By kindly deeds and virtuous life:
> Faith of our Fathers, Holy Faith,
> We will be true to thee, till death!"

When these universal movements are going on, it seems time that Scottish Christianity was putting its house in order. And the question which an outsider, such as Mr Spurgeon asks, is,—what is it that keeps Scottish Presbyterians at any rate apart? The southern intellect breaks down in its effort to grasp the Scottish state ecclesiastic.

The Church of Scotland during the eighteenth century was in all sooth broad and liberal enough. It was in 1711 that the General Assembly required every minister before celebrating the Holy Eucharist, to invite all Christians of every Christian Church to join him in drawing near to the Lord's Table. In the year 1875, the Assembly passed an act in which it was made law, that "whereas it is desirable and becoming to promote unity and encourage friendly relations among all who love the Lord Jesus Christ in sincerity and truth, but also essential to preserve soundness of Christian doctrine," any clergyman duly ordained, and holding the vital doctrines of Christianity, may occupy a parish pulpit.

The existence of the "Confession of Faith"—the English Puritans' production, which ousted the old National Scottish Confession—has for more than a century been intermittently objected to, in whole or in part, by different bodies of Christians, who have for that reason kept separate from the National Church. But let it be remembered that it and the catechisms are only the Church of Scotland's "Subordinate Standards," and that all that the Church demands of its people is adherence to the catholic truths of Christianity as embodied therein. Listen to Dr Chalmers' strong words about that Confession, which was drawn up, amongst others, by the notorious Lauderdale:—"let not that wretched mutilated document come between me and my Bible."

There must therefore be a deeper reason for the existence of the several Nonconformist Presbyterian bodies in Scotland, and especially the two largest of them, the United Presbyterian and Free Churches. It was the disastrous

Act of Queen Anne restoring Patronage in 1712 *that did all the mischief.* The Church struggled bravely against the illegal act of Parliament, which was directly in the teeth of the Treaty of Union between the two countries: but it was carried, and brought forth much fruit.

The story of the United Presbyterian Church is easily told. Towards the close of the seventeenth century, a book was written by an Oxford scholar, entitled "The Marrow of Modern Divinity," which struck against the doctrines of Calvinism—hard and stern and severe, reflecting the gloomy grandeur of those Alpine hills, in whose bosom, at Geneva, it was born. The central doctrine of the book was that Christ is all in all to the believer: but there was an apparent tendency to neglect the moral law in rejoicing in a full free gospel. Ralph and Ebenezer Erskine, Thomas Boston, the author of "The Four-fold State," and Willison of Dundee, adopted the "Marrow" views: and finally in 1720 the General Assembly condemned the book, and the two Erskines, with ten other ministers, were rebuked at the bar for what was then considered liberal thought.

Next, in 1732, the Patronage question came up. When a patron failed to appoint a minister, the Assembly decreed that the appointment should lie with the heritors and elders. Ebenezer Erskine objected, and said that *the whole Christian people should have a share in the choice of their own spiritual guide:* and, in a sermon preached before the Synod of Perth, he urged it so strongly that, at the next General Assembly, he and three others were censured. Refusing to express regret for these utterances, the four were at last deposed from the Holy Ministry, for contempt of the Church courts; and meeting at Gairney Bridge in 1733, they formally seceded and formed the "Associate Synod."

In 1761 a Mr Gillespie of Carnock objected to the intrusion of a minister at Inverkeithing, and, leaving the Church, founded the "Relief" body (*i.e.*, relief from patronage). In

1847 the "Associate Synod" and the "Relief" body united, and form now the United Presbyterian Church.

The great point to remember is that Ebenezer Erskine and his party all believed in a National Church, and had they lived to-day would have been the first to condemn its abolition, and to rejoice in its liberation from patronage. All they objected to was the high-handed and objectionable patronage of the period. The Erskines were noble men, and in their day did much to broaden out Scottish Christianity, and drive out the horrible nightmare of a bigoted Calvinism with its spiritual aristocracy and dismal philosophy. And the Church of Scotland has no little guilt lying at her door for so summarily driving these good men out, when more lenient measures would have amply established her ecclesiastical dignity and authority!

The story of the Free Church is very similar. The beginning of the nineteenth century was marked in Scotland by the appearance of the two great preachers and divines, the Rev. Dr Andrew Thomson of St George's, Edinburgh, and Dr Chalmers. Men of extraordinary power, both of them, they stirred up the sleeping Church, and again brought to the front the great fact that if religion was ever to flourish in Scotland again, the people must get back their ancient rights of choosing their own ministers. It must be distinctly borne in mind that all the founders of the Free Church in 1843 were warm supporters of the National Church. At the first Free Church Assembly Dr Chalmers said: "The voluntaries mistake us if they conceive us to be voluntaries. We are the advocates for a national recognition and national support of religion. *The longer I live the more firmly persuaded I am that the voluntary principle is utterly unfit to furnish a Christian people with* the means of Christian instruction." Dr M'Crie declared that "there is nothing that the voluntaries dread so much as the abolition of Patronage." This was proved by the tremendous opposition made by Free and U.P. Nonconformists when Parliament abolished it.

Through the Ten Years conflict, the Church was rent by the two opposing factions of those who desired Patronage and those who did not. Other questions came in and were mixed up with the main one: the old party, called the "Constitutionalists" in the Free Church to-day, still declare that they did not "come out" because of patronage, but because the State—the Court of Session and Parliament—interfered with the Church's spiritual work, insisting, for example, that ministers of *quoad sacra* parishes and churches should not enjoy the same rank as incumbents of old parishes,—and forcing clergymen into parishes where the large proportion of the parishioners were unwilling,—against the spirit of the "Veto Act."

And so the extreme Evangelical party declared that it was to assert the principle that the Lord Jesus Christ was the sole head of His Church, and that no civil power of any kind could or would dare to interfere with the Church in the exercise of her spiritual functions,—the same position as the Church of Rome assumes,—extreme Ultramontanism,—that the voice of Peter must drown the voice of kings and princes, and that states are to be the Church's nursing fathers and nursing mothers.

That sounds much better and grander, it fills the ear more thoroughly than to admit the plain homely truth that an objection to patronage made them leave the Church of their fathers in 1843; but the fact remains that when you have pruned off all that Idealism and sentimentalism, it was because of Patronage and its undoubted evils, that, on the 18th of May 1843, from the old Church of St Andrews in George Street, Edinburgh, four hundred and fifty-one ministers seceded from the Church of the country and formed the "Free Church." The real leader of the secession was Dr Candlish, and he carried away with him much of the flower of the Church.

Lord Jeffrey is said to have exclaimed, on hearing that the secession had taken place, that he was proud of the country that could boast of such a sacrifice: but then his lordship said many another queer thing, having, indeed, on one occasion used a short strong verb in connection with the North Pole, and on another, on the authority of Sidney Smith, he spoke disrespectfully of the Equator! Lord Jeffrey's opinion will not generally be considered *final in religious matters*. There was not much to be proud of, nor much to praise in a party that left the old ship, because of a *leakage*, when their clear duty was to follow St Paul's advice and abide in the ship, and help the other mariners to repair the breach which all deplored, and to *undergird* the vessel for future ages with the strong cords of popular sympathy and support, ends which have, thank God, been attained without their help.

The younger seceding ministers as they marched out of the Assembly down to Canonmills, went out, on the authority of Norman Macleod, laughing and crowing, evidently under the impression that the Old Church was done for, and that the Free Church was to take its place in the nation: the old hands, however, looked sorry to leave so glorious a past, and grave as they contemplated so uncertain a future, and in later years many of them would have been glad to get back! The last great leader of the movement, Dr Begg, held, and declared to his closing hours, that Queen Anne's Act restoring patronage had been the source of all the Church's evils!

In 1873, the objectionable Act was repealed by both Houses of Parliament, and thus the cause of all these secessions for a century and a half has been removed, to the great joy of the Scottish people and the universal benefit of the Scottish Church. Ever since that repeal, new life has sprung up in the entire Church: multitudes of dissenters, who held aloof from her because of her state bonds, have returned and are returning, thanking God for their "inheritance in a nation so great and a *Church so free!*" And, by the help of heaven, through the grace of Christ, and the guidance of the Holy Spirit, the day seems to be nearer now than it has been for many a long year, when Christ's prayer will be answered in Scotland, "that they all may be one." God hasten that day! Pray for the peace of Jerusalem!

CHAPTER XII.

"FORWARD IN THE NAME OF GOD."

The Church of the Present Day.

SIR GEORGE HARVEY's great historical painting, "Leaving the Manse," representing a Scottish parish minister and his family quitting the old ecclesiastical residence, is both telling and touching. Every right-minded person feels sorry at the sight of worth being thrown homeless on the world. It must have been with no small or ordinary sorrow that the seceding ministers of 1843, who had for long years stood before God in the Sanctuary and kept the lights of devotion alive on the Altars of our land, said good-bye to these altars for ever!

A similar event took place, though on an infinitely larger scale, at the Reformation, when the old clergy and monks were unseated, though many of them clung on to the ancient abbeys and priories, even though in ruins, like rooks whose nests have been pulled down, but which still flutter over the wood which was once their dwelling. Many a pathetic story is enshrined in the annals of the period, of the sorrowful partings which the better-spirited of the old clergy had from the stones whose very dust to them was dear.

Such partings have not been uncommon in the history of the Scottish Church: the Culdee clergy were ousted by the Roman, the Roman by the Reformed, the Presbyterian by the Episcopalian, and the Episcopalian by the Presbyterian, several times; so that while individual cases of such ejection in themselves excite compassion, on the other hand, it all depends on the rightfulness or wrongfulness of the historical movement which results in such crises, whether our compassion is logically just or unjust. A good heart goes out in sympathy with the homeless whatever may have been the cause of their homelessness: the one passport to such sympathy and compassion is poverty and need!

Now while Harvey's picture of "Leaving the Manse" excites such feelings, it must be remembered that, historically, a no less touching picture could be painted on the subject—"Left in the Manse!" In very many cases, the ministers who seceded from the National Church in 1843 were actuated by a high and self-sacrificing spirit: but an immense number of them were simply carried away in what was really the popular movement of the day, under the impression that the "Free Church" was to be the Church of the future. For a minister to "go out" was to lose the temporalities, but it meant immense popularity: to "stay in" was to be banned as a time-server, stipend-lifter, Erastian and moderate, and to be left without a congregation to which to minister, or a friend in whom to confide.

Living now in days when all these unhappy controversies have died out,—at least the *fire* of them, though there is still a little black smoke, which the general public would very gladly see better regulated, if not consumed by its authors; when a much bigger and deeper question has arisen than who was the founder of this or that sect, namely, who was the Founder of the *Universe;* when the great, awful questions of the Everlasting Yea and Nay stand staring us in the face, hungry for notice; in an age which has not made up its mind whether the Universe is a socket without an Eye, and whether the rolling worlds are Fatherless and heaven is Crownless; which is not sure whether, after all, Christ may not yet have to leave His unique pedestal in history and take His place alongside of a dozen other masters of religion in the Valhalla of Faith; and which in view of the grave and the tombstone,—that true philosopher's stone which makes everything appear in its true light,—does not regard it as the door into the Unseen

Universe, through which streams the glory of Immanuel's Land, but which, like dying Hobbes, can only mutter, "Now for a jump into the Great Perhaps:" in such an age, all the paltry, fiddling little questions which agitate the sects, are answered by the wise man, not with an argument but with a smile! As heavy sorrows save us from the tyranny of petty annoyances, so large questions cover up small ones, in the same way as the enterprising advertiser's gigantic scarlet interrogation-mark, printed across old newspapers, obliterates the thousand and one little black question-points with which the columns are peppered.

The intellectual horizon of modern life has broadened so amazingly, the intellectual telescope has lengthened and strengthened so enormously, humanity sees so much farther into the mysterious depths of space, that we marvel that what seem to us such small considerations could ever have kindled so great a fire. This broadening movement is world-wide. Not so many years ago, for a Greek priest to wear a beard was an essential of salvation. Russian Christendom was agitated over such trifling questions as whether the name of Jesus should be spelt with two "i's" or only one, whether "Alleluia" should be sung once or twice in the Oriental liturgy, and whether it was right to say, "Lord, have mercy," or "O Lord, have mercy!!!" It is no exaggeration to say that questions almost as minute have stirred the Scottish Church to its foundations; and certainly no unprejudiced mind can look abroad on the Scottish churches at the present day, without coming to the enforced conclusion that considerations quite as minute, and differences quite as microscopic, are keeping them apart at this hour!

And so ordinary people can very well be excused from taking these ecclesiastical trifles into reckoning when there are heavier questions to settle, and for turning from the splitting of hairs, to felling the massive trunks of modern inquiry which crowd in seemingly hopeless masses in front of every earnest seeker after God! And if the sects complain that busy people now-a-days, and especially younger people, do not take the same interest in " Disruption principles," and the " Claim of Right," and the " glories of '43," and so on (as many are complaining at present, and as some are endeavouring to cure, though it is like putting an infant's bootikin in front of the incoming tide), then the reply which Tennyson made to a poetaster who thought himself as good as the poet-laureate, and to ease his spleen wrote him a spiteful letter—that reply should be our reply :—

> " O foolish bard, is your lot so hard
> If men neglect your pages?
> I think not much of yours or mine,
> *I hear the roll of the ages!*
>
> This fallen leaf: isn't fame as brief?
> My rhymes may have been the stronger;
> Yet hate me not, but abide your lot,
> I last but a moment longer!"

And so in front of the great absorbing questions of Being which we all must answer in one way or another, smaller questions are passed by, and from the sinking sands of Time, with its distracting multiplicity of crooked footprints, its too many marks of scuffle and contest, its shallow rippling pools where, minnow-like, contracted minds are content to toss themselves for ever, and its shore dotted with the wreckage of a thousand exploded theories, religions, and philosophies,—you lift up your eyes to the Eternal Hills from whence cometh our Help!

It is extremely difficult therefore for us at this time of day to understand the fierceness with which the contest of 1843 was waged. After the Secession was fairly an accomplished fact, the seceding party not only triumphantly shouted, "the horse and his rider hath He thrown into the sea," but they assisted personally to put them into even deeper water and to cover "the Egyptians," as the Church of Scotland was nicknamed, with even greater obloquy! Two prominent Free Churchmen, Hetherington and Buchanan, have, like Job's enemy, "written a book," and have embalmed their bitterness in the historic page. "Every man of genius and talent," says the former, "every man of piety and faithfulness and energy and zeal, followed Dr Welsh from the Assembly." "The life," says the latter, "departed from the establishment, and those who remained, gazed upon the empty space as if they had been looking into an empty grave!" With the deepest and most worldly policy—a subtle policy which is still the most characteristic feature of the party, the seceding leaders endeavoured to carry away with them all the chapels which had been erected during the few years preceding the Secession; and when they could not do so by law, they wilfully left them burdened with a crushing debt of £30,000. Everything was done to cripple the Old Church; the new Free places of meeting were built just under the shadow of the ancient parish churches, like rival places of business; and in many places, seceding ministers made their people hold up their right hands, and swear solemnly that they would never enter the parish churches again.

One can hardly credit that the following sentence came from the pen of a Christian minister: "*You are to regard the parish minister as the one excommunicated man of the district—the man with whom no one is to join in prayer, whose church is to be avoided as an impure and unholy place ! ! !*" There's invective for you from an apostle of the religion of good-will. That injunction was studiously carried out; at Rosskeen and Resolis, parish ministers were subjected to personal violence while performing their humble duties; in scores of places churches were defaced, desecrated, and polluted, and church-members were heartlessly boycotted; and looking back from this happy year of grace on that miserable age, one can safely say that there was no man more deserving of sincere pity than the minister who was "left in the Manse!" The wonderful tide of prosperity which has of late years come to the Church, has just come in time to be some little compensation for the hardships of Secession days.

Those who can recall these days—and they are now comparatively few in number, for the generation has long passed—and who can look on this picture (the Church of to-day), and on that, marvel that the Church ever recovered from the shock. "*Nec tamen consumebatur!*" Amid a continuous storm of virulent abuse, and a worse calm of neglect, obloquy, and contempt, the parish clergy of Scotland suffered on, for the most part in the silence of sorrow and the tearless patience of trust: and once more, Keble's Scripture motto for the "Christian Year" has proved the best life-principle—" In quietness and confidence shall be your strength!" There is nothing like divine persistency and dogged cheerfulness.

It was not long after the wave struck the ship that the vessel began to right herself again. The grand outstanding hero of this age is Dr Robertson, who took up the work from which even Dr Chalmers had shrunk—the great Church Extension movement; and the result of his herculean labours was seen in sixty new parishes which before his death in 1860 he had fully equipped. In 1874, under another leader, the number was raised to two hundred and fifty. For long it became even fashionable in Scotland to underrate and undervalue the intellectual, moral, and spiritual qualifications of the ministers who remained true to the Church in 1843; but the facts are very different. It required no little principle, firmness, and self-denial to "remain in," far more than to "go out," for that was the popular move. And though few great names have come down to us of the Scottish Ministry of that period, these men undoubtedly laid the foundations of that great prosperity in which the Church of Scotland is to-day rejoicing with gratitude and humility! We know almost nothing of St Bartholomew and St Andrew, and very little of the great majority of the Apostolate; but who will say that these unknown apostles have not their place in the Temple of the Most High God? Like the vast blocks which lie at the bottom of St Paul's Cathedral, below even the crypt—unseen and unremembered, but which nevertheless are the foundation and support of the entire fabric—pillars, arches, dome, crown, and cross; so are these unknown lives which lie at the hidden foundations of the House of God.

There were, however, in the ranks of the clergy many who deserved a far greater name and fame than they enjoyed—men of faith, men of work, men of intellect, men of prayer! And, in later times, who can ever forget the magnificent labours of Norman Macleod, first in the populous Barony,—for years the greatest power in the West of Scotland,—a man beloved by throne and slum alike, and who, after evangelising the dark East end of Glasgow, threw himself into the more gigantic work of evangelising the vast East Indian Empire? Who can forget Dr Robert Lee, who stepped to the front and sacrificed his magnificent talents to the much-needed reform of the ritual and doctrine of the Church,—to whom we owe almost all that is beautiful and refined in the modern Scottish service, and the ultimate influence of whose noble life and earnest work it is hard for the most keen-sighted to augur? With divine persistency he pled for the use of hymns, for a reverent and orderly ritual in the worship of the House, for the use of the organ, and the other details of what are now-a-days considered the necessary adjuncts of a decorous worship—not only with a view to put the Scottish Church in sympathy with the other branches of the Church of God, but to check the increasing number of secessions from the Church of the country to other bodies whose only attraction consisted in the abundance of these good things which they possessed—secessions which have so happily been stopped wherever "the beauty of holiness" has been at all recognised and realised in the service of God's sanctuary. A few narrow-minded and bigoted ministers opposed him, and opposed him bitterly; but they are now all dead, and the movement which he so bravely inaugurated, and to which he sacrificed his life, has spread in a way which even the most sanguine could never have hoped! And, lastly, who can forget the noble presence, the splendid abilities, the genial, generous nature of Principal Tulloch, who, from the day that he shared the Burnett prize with the Rev. R. A. Thomson to the day when he uttered those memorable words of encouragement and warning in the last Assembly which he ever honoured,—words which, if we mistake not, Scotland will never forget,—was, perhaps, the Church's greatest pillar and ornament?

As we reach the closing quarter of a century in the story of the Burning Bush, the plot thickens, and we see the Church advancing no longer by slow degrees, but with leaps and bounds. It is within the memory of multitudes now living that our parish churches were once all empty, or something very like it. How different is the National Zion to-day with its half-million members, and, including adherents, half of the entire population of Scotland within its ample fold: advancing at the rate of eight thousand members a year, far beyond the natural increase of the population: giving of its liberality to Christian and philanthropic objects in a way which would have amazed our forefathers, to whom Alexander the coppersmith did much harm, and whose ordinary shekel of the sanctuary was the traditional "small brown," the extraordinary being a threepenny piece,—a very good coin in its way and place, but a small wheel on which to set the gospel-chariot rolling,—the largest act of Christian benevolence of modern ages being the "Baird Bequest" of half-a-million sterling;—planting new parishes and centres of work in every corner of the land, and restoring the ancient sanctuaries, hallowed by the worship of ages,—witness the magnificent restorations of the cathedrals of Edinburgh and Glasgow, and the forthcoming restoration of Dunblane, besides hundreds of similar revivals in the towns and villages and hamlets of Scotland, so that there is hardly a parish at this hour which has not done, or is not doing, something in the way of material restoration: possessed of a ministry which never in all its annals was more active, earnest, or devoted, and an enormous band of workers and missionaries at home and abroad; teaching a creed catholic yet liberal, combining faithfulness to the ancient symbols of the One Holy Catholic and Apostolic Church of which it is a true and living Branch, with sympathy, with intellectual effort and scientific advance in every direction; offering the oblation of a worship—" the worship of our Fathers," which is at once beautiful, simple, inspiring, and comforting; possessed of a spiritual independence greater than can be enjoyed in any other Church of Christendom, for even the *Scottish Nonconforming Churches are under the Civil Courts*, whereas the decisions of the Courts of the Church of Scotland *cannot be revised or reversed by any civil power ;* exercising wonderful patience under ill-natured and unmerited censure, and jealous and unchristian attack; and, above all, enriched with a panoply of grand old associations, reaching back through ages of storm and sunshine, to that memorable Whitsun-eve, May 12th, 563, when St Columba first set foot on storm-swept Iona and claimed Scotland for the Saviour! Look back: and if you are a patriotic Scotsman—if you are a well-wisher of the Scottish people, whose greatest heritage it is and the very palladium of their liberties,—if you are a Friend to Christ, His Blessed Evangel and Everlasting Kingdom, do something to keep the Burning Bush burning still, and burning even more brightly!

> " Faith of our Fathers! living still,
> In spite of dungeon, fire, and sword;
> O, how our hearts beat high with joy,
> Whene'er we hear that glorious word:
> Faith of our Fathers! Holy Faith!
> We will be true to thee till death!"

THE END.

www.ingramcontent.com/pod-product-compliance
Lightning Source LLC
Chambersburg PA
CBHW020135170426
43199CB00010B/751